PASTA
GRANNIES

VICKY BENNISON

THE SECRETS OF ITALY'S BEST HOME COOKS

PHOTOGRAPHY BY EMMA LEE

Hardie Grant

BOOKS

INTRODUCTION

Early dawn in Italy belongs to the fishermen landing their catch, cheese-makers making curds and bakers paddle-sliding dough into their ovens. There's another group of people stirring, too: grandmothers – *nonne* – making pasta for their family's lunch. It's the best time of day, they say, and for them, love is putting food on the table. In their collective past there was not the abundance and choice there is today. Food and family are to be cherished, and pasta is the perfect vehicle to make precious ingredients go further.

All Italians know their grandmothers are the best cooks, because they enjoy their Sunday lunch – or daily meal – served with a liberal sprinkle of adoration. Their nonne have cooked from scratch since they were old enough to roll dough and, by and large, only learn two or three pasta styles typical of their region. These vary dramatically from the cheese-and-butter-ladden gnocchi of the mountainous north to the homegrown tomato-based sauces served with knobbly and twisted pasta of the sun-soaked south. Some are familiar, like tagliatelle, others so obscure even other Italians don't know about them, such as *maccarones de ungia* from Sardinia.

Many nonne have their own vegetable patch, or *orto*, growing their own beans, onions and herbs – not because it is cheaper, but because it tastes better. As one grandmother, Lucia, points out, when you have good ingredients, they do the work for you. And what isn't eaten immediately is bottled, pickled, placed under oil or dried for the winter months. All over Italy there are larders and cellars full of dried peppers, tomato passata and bejewelled jars of mixed pickled veggies. Every nonna has her own recipe; in fact, every nonna has her own recipe for everything. This book brings together the cooking of these women – the Pasta Grannies as I call them. It features some of the women who have starred on the YouTube channel. The following pages reveal just how the story of that channel came about.

THE STORY OF PASTA GRANNIES

My first sighting of an Italian nonna was a pair of knees. Their owner, Maria, was sitting in the recesses of a deep veranda at the home of the Cardinale family in Serra de' Conti, Le Marche. Producers of a local wild cherry wine called *visciola*, I had spent time with the Cardinales conducting an interview, after which they kindly invited me to share a meal with them later that day. When I arrived at their home, it was one of those perfect warm, late summer evenings, the full moon turning the sky a milky shade of plum. The garden was edged with poplar trees and hurricane lamps pockmarked the night sky, providing an other-worldly glow. Our long trestle table had been positioned outside on the terrace, close to the kitchen door, and it was covered with large chilled jugs of the local *verdicchio* wine, condensation droplets forming on the outside of the glass in the heat.

It was one of the first times I had been invited into an Italian home, and Nonna Maria had cooked up a feast. First there was the antipasti: spicy, grainy Parmigiano Reggiano and slivers of young pecorino, with garlicky discs of a local spreadable salami called *ciauscolo*. Then there were plump, ricotta-filled ravioli with a simple sauce made from warmed-through diced fresh tomatoes, shredded basil and grassy olive oil. This was followed by a rich meaty dish of boned and rolled-out rabbit stuffed with masses of chopped wild fennel fronds and garlic, then braised in white wine. I couldn't believe it was the work of just one person, and not a team of expert chefs. Everyone grinned and pointed to the shadows, where I spotted the aforementioned knees. Nonna Maria was eventually cajoled to the table, but she wouldn't join us. After smiles and delightful self-depreciation she disappeared back to her kitchen.

Living in Italy – or indeed even if you don't – it is hard not to be fascinated by the nation's obsession with pasta. My neighbour's dog happily eats pasta, the electrician goes home to his mum's for lunch every day, while the plumber has a mobile kitchen in his van for those jobs too far from his own mother – although both of them are married. My local town, Cingoli, with a population of only 10,000, sustains two fresh pasta shops. It is a subject taken seriously and valued with enormous importance. Speaking with the friendly manager of my local supermarket, Alessandro, I asked him what he knew about the local pasta dishes ... and, of course, he immediately volunteered his grandmother, another Maria (now 87 years old).

Alessandro's extended family live in a row of stone houses in the Old Town. Even today, 'leaving home' simply means moving next door for a lot of Italian families. Maria's orderly kitchen was dark with wooden panelling, a central pendant light hanging in the middle and a small window. This was her kingdom, and she bustled about it, showing me little packets of frozen minced *soffritto* –

the Italian holy trinity of celery, onion and carrot, which is the base of most savoury dishes. 'I like to be organised. If I'm going to chop vegetables I may as well do it for several meals!' she declared, as she stuffed a stray bag of *cappelletti* pasta back into the freezer.

Maria was definitely the right person to ask about local pasta dishes and techniques. Having cooked for her own family all her life, in her retirement, Maria also took on the job of making pasta for one of Cingoli's neighbourhood restaurants. She gets up at 3 a.m. every Wednesday to make ravioli and tagliatelle for the weekend rush. The chef is terrified she'll retire for good.

Agreeing to show us her pasta-making skills, I invited Maria and her family to our house for lunch. Maria arrived with her pasta machine, untrusting of what I might have, and explained that she no longer uses the traditional rolling pin method thanks to the arthritis in her shoulders. Alessandro and his wife, Elisabetta, accompanied Maria, both keen to join in, and together we spent a happy few hours preparing lunch. The morning was conducted in English and Italian and everything in between, with a few games of charades when our languages failed us. Alessandro and Elisabetta were sous chefs, thrilled to be bossed around by Maria and announcing, 'We're going to do this again!' Meanwhile, I was the utilities manager, running around looking for whatever knife or pan Maria declared she needed. Aside from the incredible pasta-making technique that Maria displayed, what also impressed me was how totally unfazed she was by cooking in a totally new environment – and also that she didn't get any flour on her clothes … the rest of us definitely did. Here was a woman with many years of experience behind her, sharing the skills she had honed over a lifetime, totally at ease with herself and those around her.

Meeting Maria and her family brought home to me how Italian food culture and traditions were changing. The methods, passed down from mother to daughter (cooking was women's work by and large) over the centuries, are dying out domestically thanks to the demands of modern life. Elisabetta has a job and spends her free time ferrying her children round to dance classes and football matches, in the same way mothers do in the rest of Europe. When she becomes a grandmother, what will she be cooking? Something delicious I'm sure, but it's unlikely to be her own pasta.

By the time lunch was on the table that day, a plan was brewing in my mind. I was going to create a kind of Noah's Ark of hand-made pasta-making techniques. I would travel all across Italy, meeting the brilliant women who ran households and cook for their families. I would collect their recipes, preserving the individual methods and regional differences so they wouldn't be lost to time. The women had to be over 65 years old and be home cooks, not chefs. It would be a celebration of all women, who are too often found behind the scenes. And it would be called Pasta Grannies.

I set to work at once, finding the 'Grannies' through word of mouth, and with the help of my Granny Finders – first Gianluca Giorgi and then Livia De Giovanni. This book is the outcome of nearly five years of interviews and filming. It is a visual record and tribute to these amazing women and their families and friends.

MAKING PASTA BY HAND

The majority of the nonne I film don't bother with weighing ingredients; they have been making pasta for so many years it's second nature to them. They rely on the feel of the dough to know when it's okay. That's a bit scary if you are new to pasta-making, but the good news is making pasta is dead easy – much easier than pastry, for example. Newbies like measurements and explanation, so that's what I'm going to give, but remember pasta is not like other dough. If you use a little bit more or less flour, water or egg, it's okay. Just channel your inner nonna!

THE INGREDIENTS

FLOUR

This is a little bit of a headache because there is not an internationally agreed way of categorising flours.

00 flour – zero zero – *farina di grano tenero* – is extra-finely milled, soft wheat flour, which ranges between 9–11 per cent gluten. Gluten is a protein and that is what you will see listed on the side of the flour packet. 00 flour is what is used 90 per cent of the time when making egg pasta.

Durum wheat is a distinct species of hard wheat – and it is the hardest of all wheat species. The hardness refers to the ease with which the grains are processed, hence durum wheat flour's granular, sandy feel. The protein content is around 13 per cent, but its structure is slightly different to that of other hard and soft wheat flours, so the gluten formed is not as stretchy. It is plastic, but not elastic. These characteristics make durum wheat flour ideal for pasta making: it holds its shape and it has a nice firm bite. It is most often used in egg-free pasta – made with just flour and water. Durum wheat is grown in the more arid, southern areas of Italy like Sardinia, Puglia and Campania. The flour made from grinding this wheat's endosperm is called *semola* – semolina in English. Furthermore, you can buy it in two grades: coarsely ground, which is quite granular, and more finely ground, which is easier to use.

Heritage and speciality flours – there are of course other flours and other doughs you can make for pasta. Some of our nonne use speciality flours grown locally to them, or that they even grow themselves. In this book, these include recipes for pasta made from farro and buckwheat. In these recipes, I have included some specific tips for how to achieve the best dough, but the principles are basically the same whatever flour you use – just keep practising!

If you cannot find imported Italian pasta, or prefer to use locally produced flour, then do so. You may have to slightly adjust the ratios of flour to egg or water. Furthermore, flour behaves differently depending on the humidity, the temperature, how old it is and the company who mills it.

EGGS

Buy organic, free-range eggs if possible. Orange yolks create a more colourful, yellow-hued pasta, and this in turn is dependent on what the hens are eating. The more varied their diet, with lots of dark green leafy vegetable and grubs, the better the colour. So choose eggs from chickens who have access to the great outdoors.

OTHER KEY INGREDIENTS

CHEESE

Most of the recipes in this book call for a hard cheese to be grated over the dish at the end of cooking. In the north of Italy, this is usually Parmigiano Reggiano (to give Parmesan its proper name) and the cheese should be aged for at least 18 months. The older it is, the more granular, more savoury and more expensive it becomes.

Grana Padano is an alternative. It tends to be a bit cheaper, as the process by which it's made isn't the same (it matures more quickly thanks to a lower fat content, for example). For my taste buds it lacks the complexity of Parmigiano, but you can find some outstanding examples of Grano Padano.

Sheep's cheese, pecorino, is found all over central and southern Italy. There are lots of different kinds –

some of which are famous, like Pecorino Romano and Pecorino Sardo – and if you want to be traditional, do try and get hold of some. Parmigiano has made considerable inroads into Italy's fridges though, and you will find it everywhere these days.

Ricotta can be made with sheep, cow or goat's milk. You can also find versions with added cream (called *fiocca* in my local supermarket) in the north, while in the south it is salted and aged to produce *ricotta salata*. Fresh ricotta needs draining before use – leave it to drip in a sieve for 30 minutes or so.

TOMATOES

The majority of women we film bottle tomatoes every summer. They either grow their own, or order in bulk from a friendly farmer. The tomatoes are sieved before bottling and the resulting sauce is called passata. If this isn't an option for you (and really, that's most of us) then buy tins of whole tomatoes and blitz them with a stick blender, as Alba recommends on page 157.

Tomato concentrate is traditionally made by drying pulped tomatoes in the sun on large wooden boards or tables in midsummer. If you ever visit Sicily, try and buy some *strattu* to take home with you.

FATS

The ubiquity and popularity of olive oil has only come about since the Second World War. Traditionally, in central and northern Italy, pork fat was used in cooking as *strutto* (lard) doesn't need to be kept in the fridge. In the north of Italy, butter is used – one can even buy it in 1 kg (2 lb 4 oz) blocks. I have come to the conclusion from filming over 200 women, it's not the fat that's important for a healthy long life – it is the moderation with which it is consumed and the active lifestyle our 'Grannies' have pursued.

Olive oil is the fat listed in most of the recipes; by this I mean extra-virgin olive oil. What is more important than its nationality is its freshness. Buy it in tins or dark bottles so it keeps better and check its date of processing – don't buy if it is over a year old.

THE KIT

A smooth wooden board or table – Pasta boards have a lip under one side, which is positioned against the edge of a table or kitchen counter, so it doesn't slip while you are rolling out the *sfoglia* – the pasta sheet. The wood can be apple, ash, beech, cherry, chestnut – most woods except pine, as this has oils which can flavour the pasta and is too porous.

Your board should only be used for pasta and pastry making because you don't want the dough to pick up smells from other food. Sometimes, if our nonne aren't cooking in their own kitchens, they'll arrive with their board carefully wrapped up in its own cotton case. They are not going to risk using anyone else's board, and they don't want their own damaged in any way!

You can use marble or other porous stone if that is what you have in your kitchen. The surface to avoid is plastic, as this does not wick away moisture. I have watched a lovely pasta-maker struggle with one of those big industrial plastic boards (given to her because her husband had decided to use her precious wooden board to butcher a pig; it was a long story and she was grim faced about it) and the dough just wouldn't behave.

A long rolling pin, or *mattarello*. It should be made from the same range of woods used for the board. Combining two wood tools gives you the best possible texture to your sfoglia. It's very important the pin is not warped, as this will give you uneven pasta.

Be aware that if you use a short pin, it means you will have to cut up the dough into small pieces and roll them individually. If you attempt to roll a large amount with a short pin, it won't cover the whole sheet; you will end up with creases and, again, an uneven dough thickness.

If you are a regular watcher of the YouTube channel you may have noticed the length of the rolling pins vary all around Italy. The regions of Emilia Romagna, Umbria and Le Marche are where you'll find the 90 cm (1 yard) long pins, Tuscany less so, and then the further south you go, you will notice the boards develop edges, and the pins are even shorter as they have to able to fit inside. This is because the cooks' favoured pasta isn't egg-based, but durum wheat flour and water – and so they don't make the super-thin sfoglia.

OTHER USEFUL TOOLS

- Digital scale – it makes life much easier and you can be more precise.
- Bench scraper – our nonne often have wonderful cast iron ones made by their local blacksmith. This tool is called a *raschietto*. Alas, they are not made anymore and you will have to search the antique markets to find a genuine one.
- Large, straight-bladed knife for cutting/slicing the sfoglia.
- Ordinary cutlery knife with a serrated edge for making orecchiette.
- Grooved wooden paddle for making *cavatelli*.
- A *ferro* or square-sided 30 cm (12 in) iron or wooden rod for making *maccheroni*. Originally, this was a ginesta twig or reed, then it was an umbrella spoke – basically any straight rod that wouldn't break when being rolled. Square sides (as opposed to the smooth sides of, say, a knitting needle) stop the dough from sticking to the rod.

HOW TO MAKE EGG PASTA DOUGH

The nonna way is to decide on how many eggs you are going to use, and use one handful of flour for every egg. This handful equates to 100 g (3½ oz) of flour per egg.

Step 1: Weigh out your ingredients
Allow 100 g (3½ oz) 00 flour (or plain/all-purpose flour) per person for a main course-sized portion. You need 55 g (2 oz) egg without its shell for every 100 g (3½ oz) flour.

For example, if you are making pasta for four people, you will need 400 g (14 oz/3⅓ cups) flour and 220 g (7¾ oz) egg, which most of the time will mean four hen eggs. But weighing out your ingredients means you can also use other eggs, such as duck or turkey, which is something the nonne do – Velia on page 218 regularly uses turkey eggs as that is what she has running around her backyard.

If your eggs are on the small side, add a bit of water or another egg yolk to bring the quantity up to the right weight. If your weight is slightly over, use the egg shell to scoop out excess egg white.

Step 2: Mix them together
Tip the flour onto your board in a heap. Use your fingers to make a well in the centre, making sure it's not too wide or the rim too low, otherwise your egg mix will overflow.

Pour the eggs into the well. Take a fork (or use your fingers) and scramble the eggs together. They are mixed sufficiently when you lift the fork and you have a homogeneous, non-clumpy looking liquid that falls smoothly from your fork.

Draw your fork round the inside of the flour wall, so a small quantity of flour falls into the egg mixture. Whisk it in, smooshing any lumps, so you gradually create a batter. Repeat until you have a mixture that won't run all over the board. At this point you can cave in the flour walls and mix in the rest of the flour with a bench scraper by scraping the flour inwards and over the batter. Of course, you can beat the egg and flour together in a bowl, even with a food mixer, but it's not as fun.

Mop up any flour with your dough and give it a quick knead. If it is sticky, add a tablespoon of flour and knead it in. It is better to adjust your dough now than later.

If it is not sticky and you have some flour on the board, scrape off the excess, so you have a nice clean board to knead your dough. Nonne sieve any excess flour and reuse it.

The dough should feel soft and pillowy, but not too sticky.

Step 3: Knead the dough
Knead the dough for 10 minutes minimum. Think of your hands as waves: the heels of your hands push the dough away from you, while your fingers pull it back. Once your dough has become a log, turn it 90-degrees and fold it half and continue kneading. You want to work at a brisk pace, as air is the enemy of decent pasta – it will dry it out, so don't dawdle. If the pasta feels too dry, damp your hands with water to put moisture back into the dough.

Kneading develops the gluten and elasticity of the dough. Your dough should feel silky and smooth. When you press your thumb into the dough, it should bounce back. Some nonne judge their dough to be done when they can see small holes in the dough if sliced through the middle. To knead, you can also use a dough hook on your food mixer.

Step 4: Leave the dough to rest
At this point, place the dough in a lidded bowl and cover it to stop it from drying out. Cling film (plastic wrap) is good too, but you may not want to use it. You can also use a tea towel, but it's important it hasn't been washed with perfumed detergent as this will add an odour to your pasta. Leave the dough at room temperature for 30 minutes. This relaxes the gluten and makes it easier to roll out.

You can also leave it in the fridge overnight. The colour will darken, but it will taste the same. It's important to bring the pasta back to room temperature before you try rolling it.

Step 5: Roll out the dough
Nonne all have their own technique for rolling out. Some smooth out the dough over their pin with a dowager breast stroke in varying degrees of

stateliness; others approach it with all the intensity of a curling team scrubbing ice in front of their stone. Whatever the sporting analogy, it's most definitely an upper arm workout. Those in Emilia Romagna pride themselves in being able to roll a perfect circle. This isn't necessary but it looks gorgeous.

Julia Ficara, who runs handmade pasta classes in Rome at her cookery school Grano e Farina, recommends the following technique because it's efficient and back-friendly. This is wordy – but watching the Pasta Grannies 'How to Roll Pasta' video on YouTube will help bring this explanation to life.

Before you start, remember to keep your pasta floured throughout the process.

Cup your hands over your rolling pin so your wrists nearly touch the pasta board. Flatten your dough with your pin, turning it a few degrees at a time in the same direction; this helps to keep it circular.

When it is the size of a plate, start with your hands at hip width and roll the top third of your dough (furthest away from you) by following the curve of the circle and drawing your hands inwards as you push the pin away from you. Your hands will meet in the middle. Stop the pin before it reaches the very edge. Roll the dough four times.

Turn the pasta from 12 to one and repeat going round the clock.

You will end up with a bump of pasta in the middle. To get rid of it, flip the outer edge of pasta over the pin. Hold the pasta with one hand, and place the other hand on the dough to stop it moving. Give the pin a tug with the pasta hand to create a snug fit around the pin. Roll the dough over the pin towards you.

Move your hands wider, stick your elbows out and, pressing down, roll the pasta out two or three times. This will flatten the thicker central zone of your pasta. Finish with the pasta rolled up and turn it 90 degrees, opening it out across the board.

Repeat this process until the sfoglia (the pasta sheet, see page 17) is too large to move comfortably by hand. At this stage, you will need to roll it up around the pin and turn it, as described above. Allow your pin to roll on its own across the dough to remove any air after you have turned it.

You can let your sfoglia drape over the edge of the board – allow about a third, no more, otherwise the whole thing will slip off. This helps to anchor and stretch it, but also it means you don't have to stretch too far over the board, messing up your back. Remember not to lean against the pasta.

Do not attempt to roll the entire sheet (until you feel expert) or change rolling direction; just keep rolling the outer third directly in front of you. As the dough gets bigger, your arms and elbows start quite far apart. Eventually, you will end up with pasta you can see through. It should feel like heavy linen.

To check your pasta is evenly rolled, roll up a third, hold onto the edges (it will fall off the pin otherwise) and hold it up to the light. Darker patches mean thicker dough and you haven't rolled it uniformly, so you will want to go back over these areas.

Leave your pasta sheet to dry on the board for 5 minutes. For tagliolini, tagliatelle and pappardelle, you can now flour it, roll it up very gently (like a carpet) into a log and it's ready for cutting.

HOW TO MAKE DURUM WHEAT DOUGH

Now let's take a look at durum wheat flour and water-based dough. This dough doesn't include eggs (usually) as durum wheat already has enough bite. The resulting dough won't be as stretchy as an egg-based dough made from 00 flour. This type of dough is used for all the pasta shapes you find in southern Italy such as cavatelli and maccheroni and orecchiette. When you make a sfoglia, it's always slightly thicker and the pasta ribbons you can make from it include *sagne ritorte* and *taccune*.

Step 1: Weigh out your ingredients
Allow 45–50 g (1¹⁄₂–1³⁄₄ oz) tepid water for every 100 g (3¹⁄₂ oz) *semola rimacinata* (semolina flour). Incidentally, the volume of the water is the same as the weight: 45–50 ml (1¹⁄₂–1³⁄₄ fl oz), but scales are more accurate than measuring jugs.
   Add 4 g (1 teaspoon) salt to a litre (34 fl oz/ 4 cups) warm water. Salt is not there for flavour; it helps to make the gluten strands slide along one another better.

Step 2: Mix them together
Either use a bowl or heap the flour onto your board. Using your fingers, make a well and pour in the amount of water you need. Mix the flour into the water, making sure you mop up all the excess flour.

Step 3: Knead the dough
Knead the dough, as described for the egg pasta (see pages 18–19), for 5 minutes. You want a dough that is silky and not sticky to the touch. It won't have the soft pillowy feel of egg-based pasta dough, but it will feel nice and plastic – and you can use it immediately, there's no need to leave it to rest. If you knead the dough for longer, it will develop some elasticity and then you will have to let it rest for 20 minutes or so.

Step 4: Shape the dough
Roll the dough if necessary (lots of southern Italian pasta shapes don't require the dough to be rolled out). Keep the dough covered while you are making the pasta shapes to stop it drying out.

FREQUENTLY ASKED QUESTIONS

Why are the measurements in grams?
If you want to emulate our nonne and make pasta by eye, go for it – but watch a few Pasta Grannies videos first. But if you feel the need to measure the ingredients then I recommend grams rather than ounces or cups as they are easier and more accurate. Think of them as the support wheels on a bicycle. There will always be holes in the road: flour varies, as does temperature and humidity, so be prepared to adjust your quantities by a few grams – it's important to think about how the dough feels.

How much should I allow for a serving?
For egg pasta the rule of thumb is 1 egg and 100 g (3½ oz/scant 1 cup) flour per person. This is a generous main course-sized portion. When it comes to ravioli and other filled pasta, estimate 150 g (5 oz) of the finished pasta per person.

For pasta made with semolina flour and water, again allow 100 g (3½ oz/scant 1 cup) flour per person for a main course.

Quantities vary slightly through the book – this is because a recipe may be easier to make in bigger batches.

I have made too much, what should I do?
For egg pasta, which is uncooked, the easiest thing to do is place the pasta flat on a tray, nicely spread out, and freeze it. Once frozen, decant it into a bag or container and freeze for future use. Do not defrost it – add it directly to your boiling salted water and allow a couple of minutes extra cooking time.

Semolina and water-based pasta can be spread out and dried – the longer you leave it, the longer it will need to cook.

If you have cooked the pasta already, e.g. tagliatelle, then make a frittata or omelette with it.

Can I use shop-bought dried pasta instead?
Yes, of course. But remember dried pasta is always made with semolina flour, so if you're swapping it in a recipe which calls for egg pasta, it will give the dish a different mouth-feel. Most of us don't worry about

this; but as an aside do try, just once, to make lasagna with homemade pasta not the ready-to-cook sheets – it is so much nicer!

Dried pasta is not necessarily an inferior product to fresh pasta – the key is to find good-quality dried pasta, and price is a strong indicator (unless the packaging is very fancy). Look for the words 'extruded through bronze dies' and 'dried at low temperatures'.

What's the best way to cook pasta?
I have never seen someone use the large-sized saucepan recommended in most books and articles on pasta. I think there are a couple of reasons for this: it costs money to heat up a large pan of water – and gas is very expensive in Italy; and a large pan takes up a lot of room in a tiny kitchen. So, use the largest saucepan you have and cook the pasta in batches if necessary, adding the cooked pasta to the *condimento*.

It doesn't make any difference whether you add the salt to cold water or to boiling – with the latter you must ensure the water returns to the boil before adding your pasta. Use non-iodized, coarse sea salt and allow a generous tablespoon for 4 litres (1 gallon) water – or 10 g (½ oz) per litre (34 fl oz/4 cups) but I'm not sure most folk go to the trouble of measuring it like this.

You do not need to add oil – it's an expensive ingredient, which you don't want to pour down the sink. And, contrary to popular belief, it doesn't stop pasta from sticking; stir the pasta gently instead.

How do you know when it's done?
Nibble a piece; how long it takes to cook will depend on the size you've made your pasta shapes. Once the water has returned to the boil, allow 2–3 minutes for ribbon pasta such as tagliatelle (less if it's extra thin like tagliolini), and 4–5 minutes for filled pasta.

For semolina pasta, expect to cook it for at least 5 minutes.

Some cooks like to add a little of the pasta cooking water to make the finished dish more 'saucy'. This is a matter of judgement – it is by no means routine in the kitchens I have visited.

Meet the
NONNE

Giuseppa

When we find women in their 90s willing to make pasta for us, I'm thrilled. They can cook anything they want to be honest – the pasta is a bonus. Here are women who are still active and welcoming adventure into their lives; being filmed is a first for them. Now 97 years old, Giuseppa won our hearts the instant she opened her front door to the home where she has lived all her life. These days, it is divided into family apartments, so relatives can keep an eye on her.

'We tell her not to venture into the vegetable garden alone,' her granddaughter-in-law said with a sigh, gesturing down a steep slope to the valley below. 'But as soon as our backs are turned – she's off!'

I asked Giuseppa about her childhood. 'I don't remember real hardship, but I knew we had to eat everything. It was mostly vegetables and pulses – I still love them.'

'When I grew up, I didn't want to get married; I loved my work as a tailor too much.' Giuseppa tailored all styles of clothing, but her speciality was the traditional Sardinian costumes worn by men, with beautiful flowing shirts and waistcoats. 'And I still make the clothes for the men in my family – all nine of them. Even their underwear! They have never had to buy their clothes and I still repair them.'

I asked to see some examples of her work. Giuseppa reappeared with her wedding coat. 'I wore this over my wedding dress which had red flowers on it. I have refashioned it twice.' It is now a black jacket. 'And I still wear it,' she said, proudly.

Giuseppa did, in the end, get married when she was 34 years old – which was very old for a woman in those days. 'Giuseppe said he was attracted to me, and I went, yes, okay then.' The couple went on to have four sons – one of whom visits every day to cook for her.

'These days my appetite is small so I am not so interested in cooking, but here – I made these cookies for you!' We ate some while we showed her the video of Cesaria making lorighittas. Although the two women only live two hours' drive apart, Giuseppa had never seen the pasta being made before. She instantly picked up some pasta dough and tried to make them. 'Oh, this is frustrating! I need to make the pasta smaller!' she exclaimed, while demonstrating one can never be too old to learn something new.

Recipe: Giuseppa's fingernail pasta with tomato sauce   p. 61

◆◆◆◆◆◆◆◆◆◆◆◆◆◆◆◆◆

Ada

Seventy-nine-year-old Ada has spent all her
life in a little village called Ortucchio,
in the mountains of Abruzzo, which is
down the street from a castle that once
overlooked a vast but shallow lake.

I rather like the obscure historical
fact told to me by a local school teacher,
about the emperor Claudius who, allegedly,
when he wasn't busy ruling over his Roman
Empire in around 40 AD, used to make the
trip up from Rome to practise naval war
games on the lake because it was a good
stand-in for the sea. The lake dried up
during the 19th century, creating a flat
and fertile valley, which has become the
centre of carrot production in Italy in
the last 20 years, although potatoes and
beans are still the more traditional crops.

Ada is the youngest of eight siblings,
with one brother and six sisters. Her
parents were *contadine* - farmers - who
grew and reared a little bit of everything:
dairy cows, three or four pigs, wheat
and vegetables. Her mother, Felice, wore
traditional costume all her life, which
is something her daughters chose not to
continue. Large families were necessary in
the days before farming was mechanised,
as all hands were needed. As a result
children often completed only the minimum
necessary education before joining the
rest of the family working on the farm.
Ada completed the compulsory five years
of elementary school and was 11 when she
began working in the fields in 1951. One
of her sisters was considered so clever she
was able to leave school when she was just
10 years old.

The meal that brings back happy
memories of her childhood for Ada is
a potato and bean soup, a *minestra*, and
she still asks for it on her birthday.
It is simplicity itself: gently heat some
olive oil in a saucepan over a medium

Below: Ada's
taglioli

Right: Mercato di
Mezzo in Bologna

Opposite: Domenica
and Toni

10 minutes, until it soft and golden but
not browned. Add around 250 g (9 oz)
cooked borlotti (cranberry) beans and warm
them through with the onions. Meanwhile,
in another pan, submerge about a kilo
(2 lb 4 oz) of peeled and chopped potatoes
in water, to a depth of about 2 cm (¾ in);
if you use more water than this you may
end up with a soup that is too liquid.
Add half a teaspoon of salt and bring
to the boil. Cook for five minutes or so
until the potatoes are soft, then stir in
the bean and onion mixture. Ada recommends
serving the soup with salted green peppers
as a side dish.

   Ada's husband, Ortavio, was originally
a friend of her brother's. They met when
she was 21 and married two years later.
Together they have farmed all their lives
and continue to produce vegetables in
their *orto*, their vegetable garden. This
is a half-acre plot of land, with a two-
roomed shed Ortavio built himself. Largely
self-sufficient, they grow cabbages,

beans, onions, garlic and potatoes.
They used to keep chickens and ducks,
but a female Marsican brown bear and her
cubs - visitors from the nearby national
park of Abruzzo - raided the coop.

   'I complained to the police,' Ada
laughed. 'I said I wanted compensation.
They said we were outside the National
Park, so we weren't eligible. OK then,
I replied, can I kill the bear when she
visits again. Well, you can, said the
policeman, but you will go to jail!'
The bears seem to know they are protected
and are quite often seen on the outskirts
of the village, foraging for easy pickings.

Recipe: Ada's taglioli and bean soup

◆◆◆◆◆◆◆◆◆◆◆◆◆◆◆◆

Domenica

I wondered if the car would make it when we arrived to Domenica's. The road was unsteady and narrow; the verge giving way to nothingness and a sun-spangled view of snow-clad mountains. The hamlet near Sampeyre in Piemonte faces south, to catch as much light and warmth as it can. Chequered roof slabs of slate, the size and thickness of paving stones, clamp the houses to the mountainside built to withstand the winter-long snow. The stone steps up to Domenica and husband Toni's house have a rough-hewn dog kennel tucked under them, while the front door leads directly into a tarragon green walled kitchen, heated by a wood burning stove.

Domenica is an outstanding needlewoman. She also knits Toni's socks in intricate patterns - 'I spin the yarn too!' - and she makes his costume for a folk festival called the *Baio* that is held in Sampeyre every five years, during which the surrounding villages come together to re-enact the repelling of Arab raiders in the 10th century. This means the men of the villages get dressed up in the most elaborately embroidered headdresses, waistcoats, cummerbunds and trousers. Each village has a different style of costume and, while women don't get to take part in the parades, there's fierce pride in sewing their menfolk's finery. She also likes to make babies' christening bonnets - the girls' ones have bows on top - which she keeps in a cardboard box. 'Oh, it's sad, children are not dressed like this anymore. But look at this one; my grandmother made it.' The tiny cap is a patchwork of brightly patterned fine cottons, carefully lined, so that the seams didn't show or irritate tender scalps.

Neither Domenica nor Toni drive, and they have never owned a car. Their son brings any necessities they might need - like batteries for Toni's hearing aids - once a week from the valley below. They used to be dairy farmers and would take their herd up to the alpine meadows and live up there with them for the summer.

Selvina

The cows are now gone, but they still make the two-hour journey on foot and spend around six weeks in their electricity-free hut. 'We have just been up there to plant some beans and potatoes so we have something to eat,' explained Domenica. 'There is no set date. We go when we think the weather has got warm enough. This is the life we know. We don't want to change it.'

Below: The view from Domenica's balcony

Opposite: Selvina telling her story

Recipe: Domenica's raviole di valley Varaita   p. 110

Cremona is a strong-boned little city with a wide avenue taking the visitor directly to the cathedral, whose tower one can see for miles. It's an exclamation mark punctuating the agricultural flatlands of the Po river valley. And, just outside, in a little village scattered along what feels like a Roman road to nowhere, lived Selvina Bertuzzi. She passed away in April 2019 and I'm most sorry she didn't get to see her story in this book.

We piled into her kitchen one Sunday morning in early spring to film her making potato gnocchi. Selvina came across as shy and hesitant about making the dish, despite having cooked it for decades; her daughter, Oriana, gently helped out as sous chef. It seemed like she wasn't going to say a word, so I asked what gnocchi meant to her. And this is her story.

Selvina's father, Guido, was the livestock man for a padrone - a landowner - in Isola Dovarese to the east of Cremona. The family lived next to the farmyard of the main house. Guido received a small wage, but her mother, Santina, never got paid hers; the *padrone* could get away with it, as women's labour wasn't valued. Selvina was indignant with this arrangement: 'It was wrong!', she exclaimed.

As part of their payment, the family was able to keep a percentage of the meat they raised. Thus, they had access to eggs, rabbits, chickens and *salume* - all the different types of cured pork, which meant the yearly slaughter of a pig, which she hated. It took place in November, once the weather was cold enough.

The pig's liver, however, was

a family treat. It was chopped up and cooked in a copper pot with onion, an apple and the spices left over from the *salume* production: pepper, sage, rosemary. These were removed once the liver was cooked and it was then preserved with the *strutto* (lard) in a terracotta pot. The dish is called *frittura di maiale* and the same process was also used for goose liver. To serve it, Santina warmed the liver up so the strutto melted again, and it was ladled over thick polenta. It was so tender, they could eat it with a spoon and, she said with obvious relish, 'This treat lasted until spring.'

The war started when Selvina was six. Farms in the Po valley have very large brick barns, so the family were able to keep five secret chickens hidden in a wardrobe in one of the back rooms where the high windows were kept open for ventilation and light. The only free-range animal in those years was the breeding female rabbit, which was allowed to hop around the yard. There were the official chickens, too. Their eggs had to be given to the Fascists every week - even when they weren't laying, and that meant Guido had to barter or buy eggs. They had a system

where the older hens were the official ones, and the younger ones were hidden.

With these precious eggs, Selvina's mother would make a ciambellone cake, a ring-shaped sponge, although there was not enough sugar to make it sweet. The sugar ration was half a kilo (about one pound) a month, which was given to her father, as he needed the energy for work. He used it up by drinking sweetened milk and sprinkling it over polenta.

This meant that the children didn't develop a sweet tooth, while the adults satisfied their sugar cravings by enjoying the sweetness of beetroot, baked in the embers and then dressed in olive oil - when it was available, which was rarely. But her childhood wasn't completely sugar-free. Santina's parents, unusually, owned their own small house, which had fruit trees. It was a great treat for Selvina to climb into the attic, where the apples had been laid out on straw, to help herself to one.

Selvina was 18 when she met her future husband, Luigi, at a dance. 'I was no good at dancing, but my friends were and it was a festival, so I went along. It was love at first sight,' she said. Wanting to save for her dowry, Selvina went to work as

Below: Selvina's gnocchi

Opposite: Rachele making
her maccheroni

a *mondina* - a rice worker. This was
seasonal work lasting around 40 days
throughout the spring. A special train
collected 200 women from the area and
took them to Vercelli, the centre of rice
production in Lombardy.

'I had nightmares for years afterwards,'
she remembered. 'The first night we had
to sleep on the ground. Then the next day,
having worked for eight hours, we had
to make our own mattresses with straw
and sleep on broken camp beds. There were
70 steps from the dormitory, which was
above the rice barn, and no lighting.
It was horrible to have to go to the
lavatory in the night. The first year
there were no toilets; the year after,
the owners had dug a hole in the ground.'

The women worked a six-hour shift
in the mornings. 'We had to get up when
it was still dark...' Selvina shook her head
at the memory. Initially she wore tights,

but these were no protection, so she -
and everyone else - went barelegged and
rolled up their skirts or shorts. Planting
the rice necessitated walking backwards
through the paddy fields. 'Trouble was,
you never knew what you were going to
tread on,' she said. 'I didn't get bitten,
but other women did.' Bitten by what -
I am not sure - but the fear was real.

At 8 a.m. they stopped for a breakfast
of water and a *panino* (a sandwich); lunch
at noon was a *minestra* (soup), made by two
cooks. 'In the first year, someone used to
steal the ingredients, we never knew who.'
It was made with minced pancetta, a lot
of vegetables, like beans and potatoes,
and small square ditalini pasta. This was
also fed to the boss's pigs - they were
as important to him as his workers. On
Sundays they were given their weekly quota
of meat, while on Fridays, it was jam.

The women were not encouraged to
eat their fill, either. Their contract
stipulated a food allowance as part
payment; if they ate less, then they got
to take the rice surplus home with them.
They also received a kilo (2 lb 4 oz)
of rice for every day they worked.

After two years she'd had enough
and went back to being a full-time tailor,
making everything from underwear to
overcoats for clients. 'Everything has
to be perfect; if it's not perfect,
I'm not happy.' The role of the *mondina*
became obsolete soon after, thanks
to mechanisation along with the use
of pesticides and herbicides.

Recipe: Selvina's gnocchi with sausage   p. 119

Rachele

Sant'Agata rises 700 metres above
a bristling landscape of wind turbines.
New ones seem to sprout daily, unregulated
and unloved by the local population who
do not benefit from the electricity these
machines occasionally generate. They
are an advancing army of 21st century
technology, completely at odds with the
ancient architecture of the village.

The medieval cluster of houses are,
in fact, the more modern brick-and-mortar
addition to the original cave homes.
The houses are L-shaped: the horizontal
'burrow' and a two- or three-storied
single room vertical extension. Even
today, the rooms are connected by ladders.
Traditionally, the family's livestock was
kept in the lowest room which helped
to heat the rest of the building.

Ninety-six-year-old Rachele's home
is one of them. Her story is a gritty
Cinderella one, only Rachele has plenty
of spark and her prince was the boy next
door who never had eyes for anyone else.
I interviewed her in the old people's
home where she now lives, just above the
village and a 10-minute walk from her old
home. She decided to move there because
this was the most practical way of being
able to socialise with her girlfriends.

The second of five children, Rachele
was deemed by her parents to be ugly, and
it was therefore her responsibility as
a child to look after the donkey, rabbits
and chickens who lived downstairs. As she
had to feed and muck them out, she was
nicknamed 'Dirty' by her family. One
of her earliest food memories, aged six,
is of not being allowed to stir the cooking

pots - she could only watch her sister.

In defiance, she used to eat the
chicken's eggs. Rachele laughed at the
memory as she told me this. 'It was my
job to collect the eggs. I knew that when
they did a little dance that they had just
laid one, so I would go find it, crack it
open and drink the egg raw. When my family
asked where the egg was, I replied there
wasn't one - and they never knew because
I stomped the shell into the donkey poo!'

Rachele's mother, Maria, ran a
ferramenta - a hardware store - while her

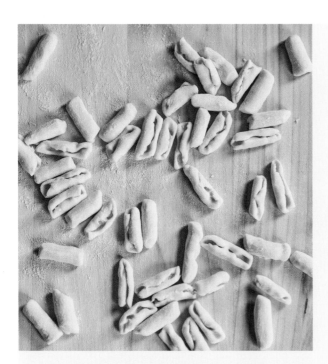

Left: Rachele's
maccheroni

Opposite: Rosa
making her
maccheroni

he was just 17 years old. He picked the
most luscious, ripe grapes he could find
and asked a family friend to give them
to her with the words: 'If you think these
grapes are sweet, think about how sweet
the man who gave them to you is.'

Rachele, indeed, found them to be the
sweetest grapes she had ever tasted, and
they were inseparable from that moment on.

Eventually, the couple moved to the
coastal city of Foggia, where Gerardo
found work on the railways. 'Those were
the happiest years of my life. We were
always singing opera around the house.'
Gerardo would go to work with half
a baguette filled with jam made from his
own sour cherries. Rachele says he also
had a passion for wine-making, stomping
the grapes with his feet. 'The resulting
wine was almost as thick as syrup - he was
the only one who loved it!'

I asked her if there were any dishes
she loved from those years. She shrugged,
'When you are poor, it really doesn't
matter what you eat, as long as you eat
something. I don't have preferences.
I do enjoy making *maccheroni a descita*,
they are fun.' Rachele likes to eat them
with a *condimento* of stewed broad beans,
when they are in season.

At the end of the our chat, I asked
her what she thought the secret to her
longevity was. She said she doesn't know,
but she thinks it might be because of her
love of family, friends and Jesus.

husband disappeared for long periods
to New York. The family speculate there
is a batch of half brothers and sisters
to be discovered in America. Maria wasn't
enthused by motherhood and when visiting
relatives exclaimed about the prettiness
of one of Rachele's younger sisters,
Maria said 'Oh, you can take her.' So they
did and a good decade passed before she
returned. For supper, Maria would feed her
brood bread and olives and the occasional
piece of sausage. Rachele remembers how
she and her siblings would suck the meat
to make it last longer.

Gerardo, her future husband, was her
only ally. He loved her from the moment
he met her around the age of six. He often
volunteered to help out in their *orto*
just to be close to her and to ease her
gardening and livestock duties. The pig
feed, for example, had to be put in a pan
and carried on her head down the steep
hillside. Sometimes, she was so tired
from working in the fields, she slept
there rather than returning home. Gerardo
decided to declare his love for her when

Rosa

There was a strange beeping noise as we stepped through Rosa's front door. It turned out she was on speed dial to her friends - she was so excited about being filmed, she wanted to make sure they joined in! Rosa loves company. 'Yes, I'm kind of well known for my parties. I put tables down the street and I make pizza for 40 or so people.' 'You have a wood oven?' I asked. There didn't seem to be space in the medieval pink-walled street. 'Yes, but I'm not going to show it to you because it needs cleaning!'

Rosa lives in the *centro storico* of a village called Sant'Arcangelo in Basilicata, high above the valley floor where her large vegetable garden and fruit orchard are. She is a market gardener - a *contadina*. 'My parents were *contadini*, so that's what I have always done. I love gardening more than I love any guy,' she chuckled. 'So, who are the men in your life?' I asked. Rosa cocked an eyebrow and nodded her head in the direction of a lone man in his workshop making baskets. 'I cannot tell you out here! We will have to go indoors.' She grinned again. The lone man turned out to be her cousin, but Rosa is a great storyteller and we all had to know more.

Rosa, it turned out, married the local priest, Don Edigio. 'He was already 20 years old when I was born. He was my mathematics teacher as well as my priest, so I didn't think anything of him. I had loads of admirers and whenever I used to present one to him and ask if the boy was suitable, he always replied, "No, no he's not nearly good enough."'

Don Edigio, meanwhile, was having doubts about his calling. He was very lonely, despite being well-liked in the village, and Rosa, in addition to market gardening, took on housekeeping duties for him. It's not hard to imagine the effect this 20-something, sparkling, pretty and petite woman had on him, who turned up on his doorstep every day to cook him fabulous meals. When their first child was conceived, he left the priesthood, married her and they had two

◆◆◆◆◆◆◆◆◆◆◆◆◆◆◆◆

Ida

more children together. 'People used to come from neighbouring villages to see my firstborn. I didn't like that, but eventually everyone came to accept what had happened. Don Edigio was popular as a priest, so people still came to him with their problems.' Rosa grew misty-eyed with the memory. 'He was tall, handsome and kind, you know. I loved caring for him and the kids.'

Disappearing into her bedroom, she brought out a large gilt-framed, poster-sized collage of her family, mostly in their wedding finery against a backdrop of a baroque church. Rosa beamed as she explained who they were and then looked a little downcast.

'They live in Genoa and Firenze,' she said sadly, which is a common experience for southern Italians – north is where the work is. So, Rosa now lives on her own, her beloved husband having died a few years previously.

But her *orto* keeps her busy. She grows everything, including horseradish, which housewives in this region of Basilicata like to grate over a meat ragù in winter. She also devotes several rows to growing the local variety of pepper, *peperone di Senise*. This is a thin-fleshed, long red pepper which everyone hangs in bunched garlands under the eaves of their houses to dry, turning them into peperoni *cruschi*. These dried peppers can be ground into a kind of mild sweet paprika, or fried in olive oil and eaten like crisps, or crumbled and scattered over food.

Recipe: Rosa's maccheroni with salt cod and dried red peppers p.147

Ida was born in 1925 and as a young girl lived in Neviglia, Piemonte. 'I had six sisters who were younger than me, and one brother. I had to leave school when I was nine because there were no more grades to attend in my village. So I started to work on my family's little farm. As soon as I was tall and strong enough, my father didn't need a farmhand anymore as I could do the work instead. I had to look after the sheep and cows, collect the hay – that kind of thing.'

'We were lucky, we always had food, and we used to keep rabbits and chickens.'

Opposite: Ida
testing her tajarin

Right: Ida showing
us her roses

This is a common practice in rural Italy where the animals are not pets, but reared for Sunday lunch. Ida continued, 'I ate everything – there was never any question of "Oh, I don't like this or that", like with young people today. Breakfast was some biscuits, maybe soaked in a little milk. Lunch was *tajarin* and in the evening it was polenta. My mum used to make ravioli on Sundays.'

Ida had an unusual war story to tell. 'We hid a young Jewish actor called Guido Sacerdote on the farm for 18 months.' He went on to become a TV and movie director, most well-known for his association with a cabaret act called the Kessler Twins. 'One day, the German soldiers arrived to check on us. I cannot remember if they were actually looking for Guido or not, but the pig had just been slaughtered. Pork meat was precious, and Dad was worried they would take the pig *and* Guido! We put Guido in the bed with Grandpa. And Dad distracted the soldiers with some red wine – and this was with all the blood still around! Eventually the soldiers left but the grown-ups all needed some grappa after that.'

'When I was 20 years old, I got married and moved here to this village and learned to cook from my mother-in-law who made *tajarin* all the time. The only way to feed your family pasta was to make it. She was an excellent cook – she made a very good *bonèt*.' (Bonèt is a typical dessert from Piedmont made with chocolate, rum and crushed amaretti biscuits. It should be up there in the popular pudding stakes with tiramisu.) 'Nowadays, I have to roll out the dough with a machine because of my shoulders, but I still cut the tajarin by hand. If you use the machine, the ribbons are not as fine.' Ida's other tips for tajarin success are that the knife blade must be sharp and thin, and that it's important to sprinkle coarsely ground semolina on the pasta sheet before you roll it, and this will stop it sticking when you cut it.

Recipe: Ida's tajarin with roast meat gravy   p. 170
Ida's agnolotti del plin   p. 240

Top: Street scene
in Sardinia

Right: Market
tomatoes

Bottom: Lucia's
son in the bakery
(p. 187)

◆◆◆◆◆◆◆◆◆◆◆◆◆◆◆◆◆

Maria

Eighty-five-year-old Maria was born and grew up in the hills just south of Faenza. Her parents were famers. 'My mum was always feeling ill with headaches. My dad was kind - but he made us kids run! I was the eldest of four, so I got the more difficult tasks. I had to get up at 5 a.m. and guide the cow as she pulled the plough through the field before school. Or else I had to make the pasta. I started making pasta for the family when I was five or six years old. Chickens were used to pay off our debts, and so were their eggs. Thus, our pasta used to have a little bit of water in it so we would use fewer eggs.

'I don't like remembering those times - the present is much better. Chickens only big enough for two people had to feed eight in those days. Mostly, we ate onions and beans because that was what we grew, and also our own wheat. We took it to the miller who ground it for us. The flour was darker then and it made a very soft pasta. Now, the pasta is better.'

Maria left school aged 10 to work full time on the farm. During winter, when there was less work to do, she was a seamstress making lingerie for an upmarket shop in Bologna. 'A famous opera singer used to buy the clothes I made!'

She met her husband at church, where the men and women had to sit separately, but the boys would parade around outside and try and catch the girls' eyes. Eventually she allowed him to talk to her and they married six years later. He likes tagliatelle, Maria says. 'I could give him tagliatelle every day of the week.'

Right: Maria with her onions

Recipe: Maria's cappelletti in meat stock   p.204

Mangia!
Mangia!

one

Nuts and herbs

I have grouped nuts and herbs together because they can both be foraged, and both sets of ingredients partner very happily with pasta. Spring is the peak time for edible wild plant hunting, before the leaves turn tough in the heat; while nuts are harvested in late summer and autumn. Try and make sure your herbs are young, and nuts are the current year's crop – it makes a big difference to the overall flavour of your pasta dish.

ROSETTA'S TROFIE WITH BASIL SAUCE

FOR 4 PEOPLE

Basil pesto or *pesto alla Genovese* is the world's second-most popular pasta *condimento*, or dressing. Pesto has now come to mean any herb-and-nut combination you can think of pairing. Rosetta and her friends add an un-classic fresh cheese called *prescinsêua* to their pesto. This has a tangy, yoghurt-like flavour with a consistency similar to ricotta. Of course, they like the taste, but it's also a way of making expensive ingredients go further. Because of this, I have called Rosetta's recipe a basil sauce rather than a strict pesto, as it is creamier than usual.

Pesto alla Genovese is usually served with *trofie* pasta, and it is only fairly recently that manufacturers found a way to extrude this shape through their bronze dies. Prior to this, the local pasta business in the little town of Sori commissioned ladies in the area to make it, and Rosetta is one of them. After she married, she wanted to earn some money while bringing up her children, and so learnt how to make it. She says it took several days of practice to get the twirl tight and the pasta all the same size; now it's second nature and her skills are such that she appears on Italian TV and YouTube (Pasta Grannies, thank goodness).

FOR THE PASTA
400 g (14 oz/3⅓ cups) 00 flour or
   plain (all-purpose) flour
180 ml (6 fl oz/¾ cup) boiling water,
   or enough liquid to bring the dough
   together

FOR THE BASIL SAUCE
2 tablespoons pine nuts, preferably
   Italian (see page 37)
1 plump garlic clove, one that has not
   developed its 'anima' or green shoot
75 ml (2½ fl oz/5 tablespoons) extra-
   virgin olive oil, preferably Ligurian
   or other grassy-tasting oil
150 g (5 oz) fresh basil leaves
4 tablespoons prescinsêua cheese,
   or live Greek-style yoghurt
80 g (3 oz) Grano Padano or Parmigiano
   Reggiano, grated
20 g (¾ oz) Pecorino Sardo, grated
½ teaspoon fine salt

TO SERVE
150 g (5 oz) green beans, halved
   (optional)

Place the flour in a mixing bowl then gradually add the water. Use a fork to make a dough that feels soft but not sticky. Turn it out onto a floured pasta board and knead it until it is smooth and silky. This will take around 10 minutes.

Cover the dough with the bowl so it doesn't dry out and leave it to rest for 30 minutes.

Pinch off a pea-sized piece and roll it outwards over the board with the palm of your hand to create a spindle shape. Pull your hand back diagonally across your body, pressing down gently but firmly on the pasta with the edge of your hand. You should create a twisted piece of pasta, which looks like a corkscrew. You can also try it with a bench scraper if you cannot get the hang of it with your hands.

Make the basil sauce by blitzing everything together in a blender until smooth. Taste for seasoning and adjust if necessary.

Bring a large pan of salted water to the boil and cook the trofie for about 2 minutes. The length of time will depend on how big your trofie are, so test one for doneness. Use a sieve or slotted spoon to scoop out the pasta once it's cooked and place in a large serving bowl. Add the green beans, if using, to the hot water; blanch for 3 minutes and add to the pasta. Stir through the basil sauce. No extra cheese is needed.

NUTS AND HERBS

It is best to make the pasta the day before you plan to eat it, as it takes a while to get into the rhythm of this shape.

PIERINA'S CRESCIA SFOGLIATA

MAKES ENOUGH FOR
12 SERVINGS

Crescia sfogliata is a kind of strudel. Pierina remembers her grandmother making it, so the recipe arrived in Fiuminata over a century ago. Strudel keeps really well, so a passing trader or returning explorer must have caused a stir in the village with this sweet gift. It continues to be celebrated: there is a yearly food festival to celebrate crescia sfogliata.

Pierina explained she uses better ingredients than her grandparents did. The sultanas were small and gritty in her childhood, and now she is more generous with the chocolate and sugar too. The latter was so precious, it was kept under lock and key in the matrimonial bedroom. The exact ingredients for the filling varied slightly from household to household and what dried ingredients were available in the winter months, when this sweet pasta is made. Start the day before you want to make the strudel.

FOR THE SWEET PASTA

1 egg

4 tablespoons mild olive oil, plus extra
 for brushing

200 ml (7 fl oz/scant 1 cup) tepid water

1 teaspoon caster (superfine) sugar

½ teaspoon salt

425 g (15 oz/3½ cups) 00 flour or plain
 (all-purpose) flour

FOR THE FILLING

5 good-quality cooking apples

350 g (12 oz) fresh walnuts (it is amazing
 how stale shop-bought walnuts can
 be – Pierina's come from her garden)

100 g (3½ oz/⅔ cup) cocoa powder

4 tablespoons granulated sugar

1 teaspoon vanilla extract

1 tablespoon anise liqueur (or another
 spirit, such as rum)

zest of 1 unwaxed orange

zest of 1 unwaxed lemon

200 g (7 oz) sultanas, plumped up in
 water, then drained

Beat together all the pasta ingredients except the flour. Make a well in the middle, then pour the liquid into the centre, being careful not to let it spill over. Use a fork to incorporate the flour gradually, beating all the time until you have a rough dough. Use your hands to knead the dough until you have a soft, silky texture. Or place it all in a food mixer with a dough hook (which isn't as much fun).

Place the dough in a lidded container and leave it in the fridge overnight. Check your fingernails – are they lustrous and long? Cut them short; this pasta will tear horribly otherwise. The next day, allow the dough to come to room temperature (still covered) for a couple of hours before you roll it out.

To make the filling, peel the apples and cut them into walnut-sized pieces. Place them in water to stop discolouration. Drain and pat dry before using.

Blitz everything for the filling, apart from the apples and sultanas, until you have a rubble-like mixture, not a paste. Stir through the sultanas.

To make the strudel, preheat the oven to 180 °C (350 °F/gas 4). Cut some baking paper to fit a 30 × 40 cm (12 × 16 in) baking tray. You will need two lined trays.

Cover your kitchen table with a clean, brightly patterned cotton cloth. (This is important as you need to see the pattern through the pasta when you come to stretch it out.) Roll your sleeves up and arm yourself with a long rolling pin – short ones will not do the job properly. Roll out the pasta sheet as wide as your rolling pin, smooth it out over the cloth and gently, oh, so gently, place your hands under the dough. Use the back of your hands and the tips of your fingers to tease the dough ever thinner. Stroke it like you are soothing the creases from ancient silk. You are aiming for a nearly transparent sheet of dough, through which you can clearly see the pattern of the tablecloth beneath. If it tears, pinch the rip together. The edge will tend to be thicker, so do a circuit of the pasta, pulling the outer 2 cm (¾ in) thinner. Use a pastry brush to oil the dough lightly.

Scatter the walnut mixture over the dough, leaving about a 10 cm (4 in) margin all the way round, then follow with the apple pieces. Turn the edges over the filling. Then, lifting the tablecloth up and over, roll the pasta over itself a few times until it reaches the halfway point. Repeat from the other side (it will look like a double scroll), see photos overleaf. Brush with oil. Either shape it into a snail, or cut it into logs and place it on the prepared baking trays.

Bake for 35 minutes, until the pasta is crunchy and coloured. Allow it to cool if you can, before tucking in. This keeps for several days in an airtight container.

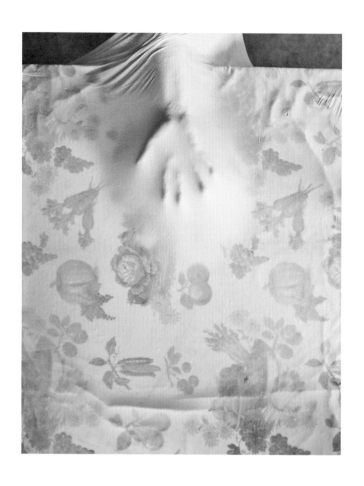

MAURIZIO'S PESTO ALLA GENOVESE

MAKES ENOUGH FOR 2 SERVINGS

Rosetta's basil sauce on page 28 is more of a delicious cream than a pesto. And I know we are keen to find out how to make the perfect pesto. Who better to explain this than Maurizio Valle, Pesto World Champion and currently a judge in the competition?

First, you need the correct kit. Maurizio has been collecting pestle and mortars for years. He has hand-hewn ancient Roman ones through to modern machine-made examples. My favourite of his was a series from a convent, which were individually marked with what could be pounded in the mortar – the nuns didn't want any contamination of flavours. What they all have in common is the mortar is made from marble – often from down the road in Carrara, where Michelangelo quarried his stone – and the pestle is made from a fruit wood, such as apple or pear, which has a nice tight, even grain.

Next, you need the right ingredients. To make the best basil pesto, you need the best basil and the cultivar is called *basilico Genovese*. And absolutely the best place for it to grow is a little town further to the west of Genoa called Prà. Maurizio has his own favoured nursery, overlooking the sea, which he thinks helps with the flavour.

The pine nuts should be Italian. They come from the umbrella pine tree, *Pinus pinea*. You can recognise them by the absence of a brown tip. They are an even creamy colour, and have a long shape. And price-wise, they will be more expensive. The cheeses, meanwhile, should be Pecorino Sardo (Liguria has traded with Sardinia for centuries) and Parmigiano Reggiano. The pesto can be mixed into pasta, soups, cooked vegetables and salads.

1 garlic clove, preferably one that has not developed its 'anima' or green shoot
½ teaspoon rock salt
50 g (2 oz) fresh basil leaves, stems removed
3 tablespoons Italian pine nuts
½ tablespoon grated Pecorino Sardo,
4 tablespoons grated Parmigiano Reggiano (18 months old at least)
4 tablespoons extra-virgin olive oil from Liguria (not a spicy one from Tuscany)

To make Maurizio's pesto, use your pestle and mortar to crush the garlic clove with the salt to make a sludgy purée.

Add the basil, pine nuts and cheeses and muddle and crush with a circular movement of the pestle (don't bash as if it were a hammer), until you have a thick paste. Then stir through the oil. 'You are aiming for a harmony of flavours,' Maurizio says.

(You could also just blitz all the ingredients in a food processor, although it will taste better and be a richer consistency if made the traditional way.)

FRANCO AND ALESSANDRA'S CORZETTI WITH FRESH MARJORAM DRESSING

FOR 6 PEOPLE

Liguria looks like it has been stapled to the mountains with the motorway that loops down its length, a rumpled shoulder seam of Italy. Its tumbled terrain is inhospitable to mechanised large-scale agriculture, and so market gardeners still flourish. Consequently, Liguria's local food markets have avoided the fate of so many in Italy, with their lacklustre stalls reselling produce from major distributors. In Chiavari there is an open-air market with banks of newspaper-wrapped posies of Genovese basil and crimped tomatoes smelling like they had been grown in soil and sunshine – for me, it's a dusty, herbal, hazy afternoon version of geranium leaves.

We had been given a tour of the town by the totally charming Franco Casoni and his wife, Alessandra. Franco is an acclaimed wood sculptor specialising in figureheads for boats, with a sideline in making stamps for coin-shaped pasta called *corzetti*. His tiny workshop is an Aladdin's cave of carvings: nymphs, Neptune faces and mermaids with buoyant breasts waiting for a life at sea.

•

FOR THE PASTA
600 g (1 lb 7 oz/3½ cups) 0 flour or plain (all-purpose) flour (it doesn't need to be the more finely ground 00 flour)
5 egg yolks, plus 1 whole egg, beaten
about 150 ml (5½ fl oz/scant ⅔ cup) dry white wine (enough to bring the dough together)

FOR THE DRESSING
100 ml (3½ fl oz/scant ½ cup) Ligurian extra-virgin olive oil or other grassy-tasting olive oil
120 g (4 oz) Italian pine nuts (see page 37)
25 g (1 oz) fresh marjoram leaves
2 garlic cloves

First, make the pasta. Tip the flour onto a pasta board or into a bowl and make a well in the middle. Add the beaten egg yolks plus whole egg. Use a fork to mix the flour into the eggs and then gradually pour in the wine. Bring the dough together. Knead until it is smooth and silky. This will take around 10 minutes. Cover the dough with a tea towel (or put it in a lidded bowl) and leave it to rest for at least 15 minutes.

Keeping the board, pin and dough well floured, roll out the dough until it is about the same thickness as a foil-wrapped chocolate coin (3 mm). As Alessandra explains, if you roll the dough too thinly the patterns from the two sides of the stamp will cancel each other out.

If you have a stamp, use the cup end of the cylinder block to stamp out the circles in the dough with a twisting motion – it's the same as cutting scone or cookie dough. Place the disc on the engraved end of the stamp block and press down with the handle. The result will be a double-sided embossed corzetto. Repeat until you have used all the dough. If you don't have a stamp, use a small glass or cookie cutter.

Bring a large pan of water to a rolling boil, add a teaspoon of salt, return the water to a boil and shovel in the pasta. Cook for 4 minutes, until the pasta tastes cooked and feels firm and not soggy to bite. Drain.

While the pasta is cooking, warm the oil in a small pan and add the pine nuts, marjoram and garlic. Leave them to bathe in gentle bubbles for 4 minutes. Keep a close eye on the pan, as you don't want the pine nuts to burn, but they can turn a little golden. Remove the garlic cloves and pour the dressing over the pasta. Eat immediately.

Recipe photo overleaf

Corzetti are typical of Liguria. The stamps and the resulting pasta have been in existence since the Renaissance, when aristocracy had their coat of arms engraved on them. Another common symbol was a stylised cross, and this is probably how the pasta got its name. These days it can be bees, wheat, your company logo, anything you like! And if you don't have a stamp, use a small glass or a cookie cutter. The discs won't look as pretty, but they will taste the same.

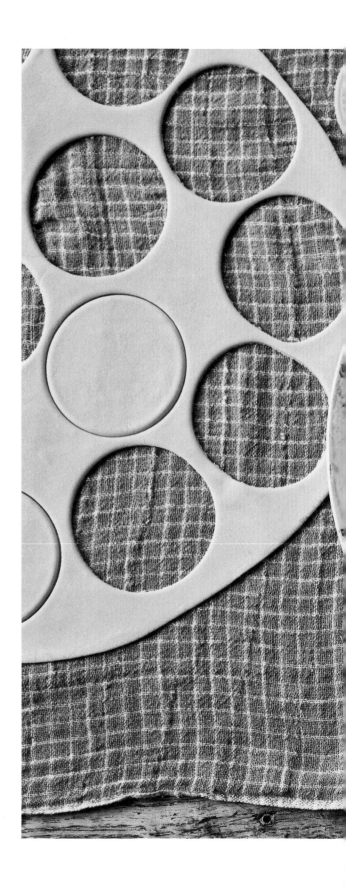

ROSA'S TAGLIATELLE WITH SWEET WINE

FOR 3-4 PEOPLE

Once upon a time, sugar was wildly expensive and only the very rich could afford it. The Venetians considered it to be the ultimate status symbol and made statues out of sugar for celebrations, as a demonstration of their wealth and power. It was the 16th-century equivalent of a gold-plated Lamborghini. Italian aristocracy so loved their sugar fix, they invented a new meal just so they could eat sweets and confectionery. It was called *collazione* and, down the centuries, this meal settled into the breakfast time slot, when Italians still love to eat sweet pastries.

For the ordinary Italian, sweetness came from fruit. Crushed grapes, including the juice, skin and pips is called grape must. At harvest time, it is slowly simmered to a syrup called *vincotto*, which means cooked wine. It was one of the few things cooks could use to sweeten dishes in the absence of white sugar.

In Basilicata, pasta ribbons (*tumact*) simmered in vincotto and sprinkled with walnuts was a treat for harvest workers. We visited Rosa in the village of Maschito, and she shared her recipe.

FOR THE PASTA
150 g (5 oz/1¼ cups) finely ground semolina flour
150 g (5 oz/1¼ cups) soft wheat 00 flour or plain (all-purpose) flour
pinch of salt
120 ml (4 fl oz/½ cup) warm water

FOR THE DRESSING
250 ml (8½ fl oz/1 cup) vincotto
1 teaspoon ground cinnamon
100 g (3½ oz) walnut kernels, broken into small pieces

On your pasta board, mix together the flours and salt and make a well. Gradually, pour in the water with one hand and use the fingertips of your other hand to mix in the flours. You want a fairly soft dough that sticks together but isn't sticky. Knead for 5 minutes, making sure you've picked up all the flour. Cover the pasta with a tea towel (or put it in a lidded bowl) and leave it to rest for at least 30 minutes.

Roll out the dough to a thickness of about 2-3 mm – it doesn't have to be super-thin like normal tagliatelle. Use a knife or a pastry cutter to slice stubby ribbons about 13 cm (5 in) long by 2 cm (¾ in) wide. Keep them spread out as you cut up the dough.

Bring a large saucepan of water to the boil, and add a teaspoon of salt. Return the water to boiling before adding the pasta. Cook for 2 minutes, then drain thoroughly.

In a sauté pan big enough to accommodate the pasta, bring the vincotto to a simmer with the cinnamon. Add the pasta, stir briefly to submerge the pasta, then let the ribbons get to know the sauce for another minute or so.

Decant everything onto a large platter, scatter over the walnuts and let everyone tuck in.

ROBERTO'S 'HAIRY' TAGLIATELLE

FOR 4 PEOPLE

Roberto Ferretti's day job is as a psychologist in the local hospital. The rest of his time is taken up with a passion for wild plants, especially culinary herbs, and teaching people how to forage and make pasta. Not just any pasta, but one typical of central Le Marche called *tajuli pilusi*. Tajuli is dialect for tagliatelle, and pilusi means hairy. The name refers to the rough surface of the pasta, created by using wholemeal flour. Roberto, in fact, uses a 50/50 mixture of wholemeal flour and Grade 1 soft wheat flour.

Obviously, before collecting wild greens you should make sure you know what you are collecting – organisations like the Woodland Trust provide great guidelines. Leaves are best when young and actively growing, so what you will collect depends on the time of year. Look for common weeds and wild plants, like nettles, dandelion, chicory, broadleaf plantain and yarrow. If your foraging takes you as far as the specialist vegetable section of the supermarket, then go for celery leaves, chard, endive, parsley, spinach, sorrel, watercress and wild garlic. Italians love bitter leaves, so include chicory or endive in whatever mix you assemble.

FOR THE PASTA
200 g (7 oz/1²/₃ cups) wholemeal flour
200 g (7 oz/1²/₃ cups) plain (all-purpose) flour
1 g (¼ teaspoon) salt
around 200 ml (7 fl oz/1 cup) warm water

FOR THE STEWED GREENS
1 kg (2 lb 4 oz) assorted fresh leaves and herbs (see introduction), roughly chopped, tough stems removed
4 tablespoons extra-virgin olive oil
3 garlic cloves, minced
1 red chilli, sliced (or to taste)
50 g (2 oz/roughly half a jar) anchovies, minced

First, make the pasta. Mix the two flours with the salt, make a well and pour in most of the water – exactly how much water is needed will depend on the brands of flour you are using. Bring it together into a dough, then knead it for 10 minutes; you want a soft but not sticky mass. Cover the dough with a tea towel (or put it in a lidded bowl) and leave it to rest for 30 minutes. Roll the dough out as thinly as you think it can go and leave the sfoglia to dry for

5 minutes. Dust it with plain flour, roll it up like a carpet, then slice across the pasta to create folded over 1 cm (½ in) ribbons. Shake the ribbons out – Roberto slides a knife under them and lets the strands fall on either side of the blade in a loose pile. Once cut, spread them out on your board.

Bring a large pan of salted water to the boil. Add all your greens and simmer for 5–10 minutes until tender or depending on how tough your herbs are. Keeping the pan of water, scoop out the greens and squeeze out as much moisture as possible. A good way to do this is to use a sieve and the back of a ladle, as the greens will be too hot to handle. Put the squeezed greens to one side while you heat the oil in a deep sauté pan over a moderate heat. Fry the garlic for 1 minute before adding the chilli and anchovies. Let the garlic and anchovy melt into each other. Add the greens and let everything stew for 5 minutes.

While this is happening, cook the pasta: bring the greens cooking water back to the boil and add the pasta. Once the water is back up to simmering, cook the ribbons for 1 minute before testing them for doneness. Drain, then heap and fold them through the greens. This is not traditionally served with cheese.

PASQUALINA AND MARIA'S TAGLIATELLE WITH TOMATO AND ANCHOVY SAUCE

———

FOR 5-6 PEOPLE

Barile is a remote little town in Basilicata where, centuries ago, Albanians came and settled – and still have an influence on the language and cooking of the area. Pasqualina and Maria showed us how to make *tumact me tulez*, which is the dialect phrase for tagliatelle served with a tomato and anchovy sauce. It is finished with a scattering of crunchy, golden breadcrumbs and walnuts instead of cheese, which would have been a luxury addition to an everyday dish.

Ideally, use stale country-style or sourdough bread for the breadcrumbs, whizzed in a blender until small but not fine – you want to keep the texture. You can throw these over any other simple pasta dishes, or use to top bakes before grilling. They will keep in an airtight container for up to a week, so it's worth making extra if you have them.

FOR THE PASTA
500 g (1 lb 2 oz/4 cups) finely ground
   semolina flour
250 ml (8½ fl oz/1 cup) water

FOR THE SAUCE
50 ml (1¾ fl oz/3 tablespoons)
   extra-virgin olive oil
2 garlic cloves
1 whole dried chilli pepper
1 tablespoon chopped parsley
60 g (2 oz) anchovies, drained weight
a glass of white wine (about 125 ml/
   4 fl oz/½ cup)
400 g (14 oz) tin whole tomatoes, broken
   up using the back of a spoon
500 g (1 lb 2 oz) tomato passata
   (sieved tomatoes)
25 g (¾ oz) fresh basil leaves
½ teaspoon salt (but taste first,
   remembering the anchovies can
   be quite salty)

FOR THE BREADCRUMB DRESSING
1-2 tablespoons extra-virgin olive oil
100 g (3½ oz) breadcrumbs
   (see introduction)
1 garlic clove, minced (optional)
50 g (2 oz) finely chopped walnuts
2 tablespoons chopped parsley

Make the dough, as described on page 21. Let it rest.

Warm the oil in a sauté pan over a moderate heat and add the whole garlic cloves, chilli pepper, parsley and anchovies. Fry for 5 minutes, so that the anchovies dissolve.

Splash in the wine and let it evaporate. Next, stir in the tinned tomatoes and passata. Add the whole basil leaves. Taste, and season if you think the sauce needs salt. Leave it to reduce for 10 minutes or so.

Next, make the dressing. Take a large frying pan (skillet), add a splash of olive oil, and heat it over a high heat for a couple of minutes. Add the breadcrumbs and fry them, stirring constantly, until the crumbs have turned crunchy and golden. If you like garlic, stir through a minced clove as the breadcrumbs start to turn colour. Shovel everything into a shallow bowl – the crumbs will cool more quickly. Once cold, mix in the walnuts and parsley.

To make the pasta, roll out the dough so it's about 1-2 mm thick. Pasqualina and Maria demonstrated three different widths of tagliatelle – this tells you the style is yours to choose, but be consistent, so the pasta strands all cook evenly. The fastest and prettiest method is to take a pastry cutter (for a frilled edge) and cut 1 cm (½ in) wide ribbons.

Bring water to the boil in a large saucepan, add a couple of teaspoons of salt, and return the water to the boil. Add the pasta all at once, give it a stir, and cook for a couple of minutes. Nibble a strand to test for doneness. Drain thoroughly.

Remove the garlic cloves, chilli pepper and basil leaves from the sauce. In a large serving bowl, layer the ingredients: breadcrumb dressing, pasta and sauce, repeating as necessary. Eat immediately.

CORNELIA'S PANSOTTI WITH WALNUT PESTO

FOR 4–5 PEOPLE

Cornelia's home is perched high above the Ligurian coastline surrounded by olive trees clinging to near vertical slopes, and whose branches provide hazy shade for the curtain-falls of wild flowers in spring. She is an enthusiastic forager for the posy of herbs needed to make *pansotti*. 'You need at least seven varieties of herbs,' she says. 'You must pick them while they are young and still growing, and you want a balance of flavours. Some, like the dandelions, are bitter. Borage has a cucumber flavour, but there are others like nettle, *campanula* and *Sanguisorba* which are mild, too.' This is called *preboggiòn* locally, and the composition varies according to the forager, the location and the time of year.

In Liguria, you will find ready-made bunches in the markets. It would be a shame not to make these ravioli because you don't have the right herbs. Use a mixture of spinach, watercress and rocket (arugula) instead – and maybe something like a red chicory to make the flavour a bit punchier.

FOR THE PASTA
400 g (14 oz/3⅓ cups) 00 flour
   or plain (all-purpose) flour
1 egg
1 tablespoon extra-virgin olive oil
about 150 ml (5 fl oz/⅔ cup) water

FOR THE FILLING
500 g (1 lb 2 oz) mixture of green leaves
   (see introduction)
3 teaspoons fresh marjoram leaves
1 garlic clove, crushed in a little salt
1 tablespoon extra-virgin olive oil
1 egg, beaten
50 g (2 oz) Parmigiano Reggiano

FOR THE WALNUT PESTO
50 g (2 oz) breadcrumbs (see page 47)
about 300 ml (10 fl oz/1¼ cups) milk
100 g (3½ oz) walnuts
50 g (2 oz) Italian pine nuts (see page 37)
1 garlic clove
3 teaspoons fresh marjoram leaves
salt and pepper

Make the pasta dough as described on page 18. Leave it to rest while you make the filling.

Blanch the greens in a large pan of boiling salted water for a few minutes. Drain and squeeze the mixture dry as soon as it is cool enough to handle.

You should end up with around 270 g (10 oz) of cooked leaves. Chop them up until it is nice and mushy. Mix with the remaining ingredients.

To make the pansotti, roll out the dough to about 1 mm thickness (i.e. quite thin). Cut a grid of 5–6 cm (2 in) squares. Add a teaspoon of filling to each square and fold the square over to form a triangle. Press the edges firmly together, then bring the two small-angled corners together and press the points. They should point away from the other corner, and the pansotti should look bulbous; pansotti means belly in Ligurian.

To make the walnut pesto, first soak the breadcrumbs in the milk and squeeze out any excess – keep the milk so you can add it when you blitz the ingredients. Preheat your oven to 140°C (275°F/gas ½) and spread the walnuts and pine nuts across two separate baking trays. Toast them for 10 minutes until golden and fragrant. One set of nuts may cook quicker than the other so keep an eye on them. Leave to cool, then blitz in a high-speed blender with the rest of the pesto ingredients, adding enough milk for it to reach a luscious and quite thick consistency, similar to a slightly runny hummus. Season to taste, adding more marjoram if you like.

Bring a large pan of salted water to the boil and simmer the pansotti for 5 minutes. Drain them and then dress with the pesto. Any leftover pesto can be used as a dip or spooned over vegetables or poached chicken.

ANGELA'S BUSIATE WITH TRAPANESE PESTO

FOR 6 PEOPLE

Angela is a farmer's wife whose family grow wheat. Most recently, they have reintroduced a heritage durum wheat variety, special to Sicily, called *Perciasacchi*, which she uses to make *busiate*, a twizzled maccheroni typical of the Trapani province in the west of Sicily. The name comes from the Sicilian word *busa*, which is the dried stem of a local grass (*Ampelodesmos mauritanicus* for any botanists reading this), which is used to make the pasta. You will need something similar: a length of dowling, a bamboo skewer, or a comparable item.

For pesto Trapanese, Angela recommends one garlic clove per person. In Salemi, the pesto was traditionally a mash of garlic, tomato and basil, but more recently they have adopted a Trapanese habit of adding almonds and pine nuts to the mix. The resulting pesto doesn't have the vibrant green look of pesto Genovese (see page 37), but add this to your summer repertoire anyway.

FOR THE PASTA

500 g (1 lb 2 oz/4 cups) finely ground semolina flour (if you can, use a heritage flour like Angela's)
250 ml (8½ fl oz/1 cup) tepid water
2 g (½ teaspoon) salt

FOR THE PESTO

16 medium ripe and flavoursome tomatoes
6 garlic cloves (or to taste)
1 teaspoon salt
8 sprigs of basil, leaves only
20 g (¾ oz) skinned whole almonds
10 g (½ oz) Italian pine nuts (see page 37)
about 50 ml (1¾ fl oz/3 tablespoons) extra-virgin olive oil

Make the pasta dough as described on page 21. Cut the dough in half and roll each piece into a disc about 1 cm (½ in) thick. Slice these into ribbons about 1 cm (½ in) wide and roll each out one to the thickness of your mobile (cell) phone charging cable. You want them to be about 20 cm (8 in) long, so cut them in half or thirds.

To make the busiate, place a pasta length 12 to 6 o'clock on the board, then take your rod and put it at a 45-degree angle at the 12 o'clock end with your left hand. Use your other hand to press the stick into the pasta and roll it towards you so the pasta begins to spiral around the stick. Once the pasta is twirled, gently roll it with the palm of your right hand to flatten it a bit. Don't press too hard or it will stick together and to the rod. Hold the stick upright and the pasta should slip off. Repeat until you have used all the pasta. You can leave them to dry and use them the following day, if you wish.

Skin the tomatoes. Angela uses what I call a 'nonna knife' – a serrated, plastic-handled number – to peel them like an apple. Or jab the tip of a knife into each tomato and drop them into boiled water. Leave them for 5 minutes and take the skin off with your fingers, as soon as they are cool enough to handle. Chop them up, making sure not to lose all the juices.

To make the pesto, you can take the easy road and pulse all the ingredients except the oil together in a food processor, making sure you still have a crunchy, rubble-like texture to the pesto. Then stir through the oil.

If you have a pestle and mortar, crush the garlic cloves with the salt. Add the basil leaves, almonds and pine nuts and pound them until the almonds are definitely at the smithereens stage of demolition. Add the chopped tomatoes and give everything a good muddle, then stir in the oil.

Bring a large pan of salted water to the boil. Drop the busiate into the water and once it has returned to the boil, cook them for around 6 minutes – how long will depend on the thickness of your busiate. The best way to tell is to nibble one.

Drain the pasta and dress it with the pesto. The tomato juices mean you are unlikely to need the pasta water for the pesto. This is a no-cheese pasta dish. Serve immediately.

two

Vegetables

This chapter is not strictly vegetarian, and in it you will find several recipes that include a little meat. This is because the notion of being a vegetarian is an alien concept to the women we film, even though most of what they eat could be described as that. Meat is precious, a food to be eked out and cherished, so you will find the occasional sausage or slice of pancetta in the sauces here. Of course, omit the meat if you wish. Instead, think of this chapter more as a celebration of vegetables.

Most importantly, try and buy vegetables when they are in season locally. And if you do not make your own tomato passata (sieved tomatoes), make sure to use a good-quality brand.

MARGHERITA'S CAVATI WITH SPRING VEGETABLES

FOR 4–6 PEOPLE

Margherita is the mother of chef Carmelo Chiaramonte, who is well known in Italy as a sort of wandering troubadour cook, always lauding the links between food and love, while producing the most wonderful plates of food from the simplest of ingredients. Margherita quite often appears as his sous-chef-cum-sidekick, and she has developed a theatrical style of making her dough, thumping it down with gusto.

Home for Margherita is in the hills overlooking Modica, Sicily, surrounded by pastures where wild asparagus and fennel grow in early spring. If you like foraging and are lucky enough to find a few sprue, then this is the pasta dish for you. I have given measurements, but to be honest, you can vary the ingredients and quantities to what's available in your garden or farmers' market – just try to make sure the vegetables are young and fresh. If you don't have fresh fennel to hand, use parsley.

This dish involves creating as much flavour as possible by first creating a stock from the vegetable waste, then simmering the vegetables in it. Oil is only added as a dressing at the end. Carmelo says this is typical of farmhouse cooking of the area.

FOR THE PASTA
400 g (14 oz/3⅓ cups) finely ground semolina flour
200 ml (7 fl oz/1 cup) tepid water
2 g (½ teaspoon) salt

FOR THE SAUCE
1 kg (2 lb 4 oz) broad (fava) beans (unpodded weight)
400 g (14 oz) fresh peas in their pods
250 g (9 oz) thin asparagus
4 large artichokes
1 small leek or big spring onion (scallion)
1 small bunch of wild fennel fronds
150 g (5 oz) ricotta
salt

TO SERVE
extra-virgin olive oil, to drizzle

Pod your broad beans – a kilo (2 lb 4 oz) should give you around 300 g (10½ oz). Keep the pods. Do the same with your peas – you should end up with around 200 g (7 oz) peas. Trim the woody ends off the asparagus, then chop into 4 cm (1½ in) batons. Prepare the artichokes as described on page 72 (leave the stalks intact, and the artichokes unsliced). Remove any papery skin from the leek and chop up.

Place all your trimmings and pods in a large saucepan and cover with water. Season with salt, cover the pan and simmer for 40 minutes. Scoop out and discard the debris. Use this stock to simmer all the vegetables, adding the fennel fronds. Simmer until all the vegetables are tender – 30 minutes or so.

Make the pasta dough as described on page 21. Roll out the dough so the sfoglia is about 6–7 mm (¼ in) thick. Cut it into strips the width of your middle three fingers (4–5 cm/1½–2 in) and then pile them on top of each other and cut into batons, just under 1 cm (½ in) wide. Plant your three middle fingers into a baton and roll it towards you. You are aiming for something that looks like a pea pod.

Bring a large pan of salted water to the boil and cook the pasta for around 5 minutes. Drain the pasta. Add the ricotta to a serving bowl, and scoop the cooked vegetables into the ricotta. Mix everything together, stirring in a little more veg stock, if necessary, and then fold through the pasta. Drizzle extra-virgin olive oil over each serving.

MARIA'S RASCHIATELLI WITH RED PEPPERS

———

FOR 4 PEOPLE

Maria and her husband are farmers, growing a mixture of vines and wheat. Maria says, 'We own this farm, but my parents were farm labourers and worked in the fields every day. I think, when I was about eight years old, they asked me to have the pasta ready when they came home. And that was that. I have made *raschiatelli* ever since. The more there are of you, the bigger your raschiatelli can be – look at this one. This is called ten-digits in dialect.' Maria planted all of her fingers and thumbs into a rope of dough and pulled it across the board. 'They are nearly the size of broad (fava) bean pods, but it's a quick way to feed large numbers of people.'

A keen vegetable gardener, Maria's plot in mid-summer is full of lush tomato and pepper plants in regimented rows. 'The key to being good at gardening is to give your plants lots of love, starting with the soil.' Her peppers are a variety called *peperone di Senise* – a thin walled, long, slightly dented-looking red pepper, which is very sweet. In summer, the shaded eaves of her house are garlanded with drying peppers. It's unlikely you'll find the Senise peppers in your local market, so choose any long red pepper, for example, Romano.

FOR THE PASTA
400 g (14 oz/3⅓ cups) finely ground semolina flour
180–200 ml (6–7 fl oz/scant 1 cup) tepid water
2 g (½ teaspoon) salt

FOR THE SAUCE
2–4 long red peppers (depending on their size)
3–4 tablespoons extra-virgin olive oil
2 garlic cloves, sliced
6–7 ripe, large flavoursome tomatoes
bunch of basil
salt

TO SERVE
grated ricotta salata

Make the pasta dough as described on page 21. Cut the dough into apricot-sized pieces and roll them out into ropes about the thickness of an asparagus spear, or something similar to this - nothing too spindly or chunky - unless you want your raschiatelli to turn out like that, of course.

Maria's raschiatelle are three-fingers long, so measure your first three fingers on a pasta rope and cut pieces accordingly. To make the shape, put your fingers on the outside edges of a dough piece and pull your fingers across it, pressing down as you do so. Maria rolls them with both hands at the same time for speed. You can leave them to dry once made, but remember they will take longer to cook.

To make the sauce, strip out the pith from the peppers and slice them finely. Warm the olive oil in a sauté pan over a low to medium heat. Chuck in the peppers with the garlic and let the mixture soften without caramelising, stirring often; this will take about 10 minutes.

Chop up the tomatoes, add them to the pan with a pinch of salt, and stew everything until you have a thick, sludgy sauce, which will take around 25 minutes. Add a little water if the vegetables haven't collapsed enough by the time the juices have evaporated. This sauce can be made ahead of time if that is more convenient for you.

Strip the basil leaves off their stalks and stir them through.

Bring a large pan of salted water to the boil and add the pasta. When they bob to the surface, simmer them for 4–5 minutes; how long will depend on the size of your raschiatelli. Test one to check for doneness. Drain the pasta.

Toss the raschiatelli with the sauce, check the seasoning and plate up with plenty of grated ricotta salata over each serving.

GIUSEPPA'S FINGERNAIL PASTA WITH TOMATO SAUCE

———

FOR 4 PEOPLE

Ninety-seven-year-old Giuseppa lives in the village of Ozieri, Sardinia, where the local pasta shape is *macarrones de ungia*, which means fingernail pasta.

Giuseppa uses a curved strip of punctured metal which hugged the side of her table to make her macarrones de ungia. If you are prepared to visit Ozieri's weekly market, you may be lucky and find one; otherwise, the back of a nutmeg grater is a good substitute. Giuseppa told me that other villages in the area use different implements like pieces of rough glass, or tile, and of course grooved wooden paddle shaped boards. But try a nutmeg grater; the resulting pasta pieces look like tiny raspberries. These are easy and fun to make!

FOR THE PASTA
400 g (14 oz/3⅓ cups) finely ground semolina flour
200 ml (7 fl oz/scant 1 cup) tepid water
2 g (½ teaspoon) salt, dissolved in the water

FOR THE SAUCE
1 onion, roughly chopped
1 garlic clove
3 tablespoons extra-virgin olive oil
20 g (¾ oz) bunch of parsley
3 sprigs of basil
500 g (1 lb 2 oz) passata (sieved tomatoes) or chopped fresh tomatoes
salt

TO SERVE
grated Pecorino Sardo
fresh basil, only leaves

Make the pasta dough as described on page 21. Take small chunks off the dough and roll them out to the thickness of a wax crayon. Pull peanut-sized pieces off the rope and roll them over the back of a nutmeg grater to create knobbly little gnocchi. Giuseppa gave me the pasta she made – I still have the full jar, because it seems to me to be a work of art and impossible to eat.

Make the tomato sauce by softening the onion and garlic in the olive oil in a saucepan. Add the parsley, basil and passata to the pan, season with a little salt and leave everything to simmer for 20 minutes. Pass the sauce through a food mill or blitz it with a hand-held blender to incorporate the herbs, onion and garlic.

Bring a large pan of salted water to the boil then roll down to a simmer. Pour in the macarrones and bring the water back to the boil. Test for doneness after 3 minutes; keep simmering for another minute or so if not ready.

Drain the pasta and as you shake it onto a serving platter, sprinkle grated Pecorino through it. Plate up and dress each serving with some sauce and a few basil leaves.

MARIA'S SAGNE WITH BROCCOLI AND TOMATO SAUCE

FOR 4 PEOPLE

Maria has lived for her whole life just outside Lecce, Puglia, in the very south of Italy. She was 13 when she started making pasta and was given the weekly task of taking the family's bread to the bakers. Her mum loaded 16 kg (over 35 lb) of dough onto a long plank and Maria had to carry it across her shoulder and unload it for the baker to cook. This quantity kept eight people fed for an entire week.

Italians love their greens, and while you may have heard of *cime di rape*, you probably haven't come across *mugnuli* – which is also called *broccoletti salentini* in Italian. Like its more famous cousin, mugnuli is a brassica. It is found in the Salento region of Puglia, as well as Campania.

'Well,' said Maria, 'it's similar to sprouting broccoli but the flower heads are small and loosely packed, and the flowers are white – although if you see that, then you have left it too late to pick them.' We stood in her kitchen, peering into her concrete kitchen sink the size of a small bathtub, filled with greenery. 'You only use the flower heads and tender stalks. The flavour is soft – something like broccoli, but also cauliflower. It's spontaneous – it grows wild – but I can buy it, too.' This recipe is one she makes in the short season that mugnuli is available – it doesn't like warm weather. For those of us who do not live in southern Italy, sprouting broccoli is an acceptable substitute.

FOR THE PASTA
400 g (14 oz/3⅓ cups) finely ground
    semolina flour
180–200 ml (6–7 fl oz/¾–1 cup)
    warm water
2 g (½ teaspoon) salt

FOR THE BROCCOLI AND TOMATO SAUCE
3–4 tablespoons extra-virgin olive oil
1 onion, sliced
6 ripe and flavoursome tomatoes,
    chopped
400 g (14 oz) mugnuli or broccoli stems
salt

TO SERVE
chilli oil (optional)
grated ricotta salata

Make the pasta dough as described on page 21. Roll out the dough until it is about 2–3 mm thick. Cut into 2 cm (¾ in) wide ribbons. To make the sagne, hold one end of a ribbon down on the board and roll it twice with the palm of your other hand, to make a long spiral. If it's very long, turn the ribbon around and give the other end a twist. Fold it in half and place it on a tea towel-covered tray. The pasta can be left like this for several hours. This is a good pasta for getting children involved.

To make the sauce, heat the olive oil in a sauté pan. Soften the onion in the oil, which will take about 7 minutes. Stir in the tomatoes and cook them for about 20 minutes, until they have collapsed and you have a thick sauce. Season it with salt. Add the broccoli and simmer until it is properly soft, adding a dribble of water when necessary. This will take a good 15 minutes. You want a chunky mush – which is not how lots of people like to cook their broccoli, but the sauce needs to cling to the pasta.

Bring a large pan of salted water to the boil and cook the sagne for about 5 minutes: how long will depend on the size of your ribbons and the length of time you left them to dry. Taste one to check. Drain the paste and add it to the pan with the sauce. Toss with the sauce and plate up. Serve with chilli oil, if you like, and plenty of grated ricotta salata.

GAIA'S CULURGIONES WITH TOMATO SAUCE

**MAKES 50 CULURGIONES,
ENOUGH FOR 10 PEOPLE**

Our brief for finding women (and men) for the Pasta Grannies YouTube channel is they have to be over 65. But we make exceptions, and Gaia is one of them because she is such a whizz at making *culurgiones*. Only, in her village of Escalaplano, in southeast Sardinia, they are called *culixionisi a spighetta*. 'Spighetta' refers to the way the ravioli is closed, making it look like an ear of corn. The spelling, size and fillings vary from village to village, but culurgiones always include mashed potato. They are made on special occasions, like the end of harvest and the Day of the Dead (1 November), and they are given to others as a symbol of friendship.

'I started to make pasta when I was really young, like 5 years old,' Gaia told us, 'with my grandmothers, nonna Massimina and nonna Maria, who are both from Escalaplano. They encouraged me to play with the pasta, like it was a game, and I thought it was really good fun, especially since I got to play with them, too! When I was 19, I became really interested in learning my grandmothers' pasta secrets, so I asked nonna Massimina to teach me. She always said, "Close the culurgiones with a very fine and dense seam, almost as though you are sewing by hand, with a lot of patience and commitment."

'And she was thrilled when she saw the Pasta Grannies video with me – she loved that her teaching was reaching the wider world. Unfortunately, she passed away in September 2018, and that's why I want to dedicate this page in her memory. Thank you, Nonna Massimina, for all your love and inspiration.'

This recipe makes about 50 culurgiones – enough for 10 people if they are not going to have a second course. They freeze well though – cook them straight from frozen – and you can also halve the quantities if you wish.

Recipe method overleaf

FOR THE PASTA

1 kg (2 lb 4 oz) finely ground semolina
   flour
450–500 ml (15–17 fl oz/2 cups) water
1 tablespoon extra-virgin olive oil
8 g (2 teaspoons) salt

FOR THE TOMATO SAUCE

1 onion, diced
3–4 tablespoons extra-virgin olive oil
1 kg (2 lb 4 oz) passata (sieved tomatoes)
20 g (¾ oz) fresh basil leaves, plus extra
   to serve
½ teaspoon salt

FOR THE FILLING

1 kg (2 lb 4 oz) potatoes
100 g (3½ oz) aged Pecorino, finely
   grated
200 g (7 oz) fresh Pecorino, finely grated
200 g (7 oz) fresh soft goat's cheese
4 tablespoons freshly chopped mint
1 egg, beaten
2 garlic cloves, minced to a pulp with
   a pinch of salt
4 tablespoons extra-virgin olive oil
pinch of powdered saffron (optional)

Make the pasta dough as described on page 21. Not everyone puts oil into the dough, but for Massimina it was very important. Set it aside to rest.

Make the tomato sauce by softening the onion in olive oil in a saucepan, then adding the passata, whole basil leaves and salt. Leave the mixture to simmer for 30 minutes and remove the basil at the end of cooking.

While the sauce is cooking, roll out the dough to about 2 mm thick. Use a cookie cutter to make circles in the dough, 8 cm (3 in) in diameter. Keep them covered with just-damp tea towels to stop them from drying out.

To make the filling, peel, quarter and boil the potatoes. When cooked, after 15 minutes or so, drain them thoroughly, then mash them. Once the potatoes have cooled to lukewarm, thoroughly mix all the filling ingredients together.

Add a walnut-sized dollop into the centre of each pasta circle. Cup one in your left hand (if you are right handed) and 'sew' the seam across the top, starting at one end of the half-moon with the tips of your thumb and forefinger of your other hand. It is an alternate pleating motion, bringing one side over the other (watching Gaia do it on the video is very helpful to understand what's happening!). Remember, it will taste the same even if you get it wrong the first few times you try. Don't worry if some filling creeps out towards the end of the process either – it means you have created plump culurgiones.

Bring a large pan of salted water to the boil and cook the culurgiones in batches. Once they bob to the top – which will take around 5 minutes – you can scoop them out and dress them in the tomato sauce and basil leaves.

FELICA'S BASIL PASTA WITH AUBERGINE SAUCE

FOR 4 PEOPLE

Felica runs a little general store – with an excellent wine cellar – high above the shoreline in the village of Praiano on the Amalfi Coast. It has to be a contender for the supermarket-with-the-best-view award! This is a favourite recipe of hers because 'all my family love it'. Indeed, her son hovered in the background waiting for the finished dish.

The secret ingredient is the *provola affumicata*, a smoked mozzarella-style cheese, which turns stringy and delicious as it melts into the sauce. Most good Italian delis should stock it.

If you can't find provola affumicata, then try this with scamorza, smoked mozzarella, or even burrata – the latter won't have the same flavour, but will be delicious all the same.

FOR THE PASTA
200 g (7 oz/1²/₃ cups) 00 flour or plain (all-purpose) flour
200 g (7 oz/1²/₃ cups) finely ground semolina flour
3 eggs, beaten
3 tablespoons milk
1 tablespoon extra-virgin olive oil
4 tablespoons shredded basil

FOR THE SAUCE
1 large aubergine (eggplant)
vegetable oil, for frying
2 tablespoons extra-virgin olive oil
1 small onion, finely diced
400 g (14 oz) flavoursome sun-ripened tomatoes, chopped
200 g (7 oz) (one ball) of provola affumicata, roughly chopped (see introduction for other varieties)
salt

TO SERVE
a handful of torn basil leaves
2 tablespoons grated Parmigiano Reggiano

On a wooden board, mix the two flours together and make a well. Pour the eggs into the middle, along with the milk, oil and basil. Use your fingers to mix the liquids together and then gradually incorporate the flour. Knead it until it is smooth and leave it to rest, covered with a tea towel (or put it in a lidded bowl), for 30 minutes.

Peel the aubergine and cut it into 2 cm (¾ in) cubes. Salt them lightly and place them in a sieve over the sink for 30 minutes. Rinse off the salt and leave them to dry in the sun or pat them dry with a tea towel. (Or, skip this step if you are confident your aubergine won't taste bitter.)

Splash a little vegetable oil into a large non-stick frying pan (skillet) and warm it up over a moderate to high heat, before adding the aubergine cubes in a single layer. If your frying pan is small, cook the aubergine in batches. Stir the cubes regularly until they develop a golden-brown colour. Don't add any more oil, as you'll end up with soggy aubergine. (Aubergine cooked in this way is called a *funghetto* in Italian, which means 'in the style of mushrooms'.)

In another pan, soften the onion in a little olive oil over a medium heat, which will take around 7 minutes. Add the tomatoes and let everything simmer and collapse into a mush.

While that is happening, return to your pasta. Keep the board well floured and roll the dough out to about 2 mm thick. Roll it up like a carpet, then cut across the pasta to create folded over ribbons about 1 cm (½ in) wide. Keep the ribbons well distributed to stop them sticking.

Bring a large saucepan of salted water to the boil and add your pasta. Cook for 2 minutes. Drain, keeping a ladle of pasta water in case you want to make your dish more saucy at the end.

Add the pasta to the tomatoes, along with the aubergine and chopped cheese, and fold everything together. A pair of salad servers is good for this task.

Scatter over some torn basil leaves and grated Parmigiano Reggiano, and serve immediately.

MARIA LUISA AND MENA'S FETTUCCINE WITH ARTICHOKES

———

FOR 4 PEOPLE

Maria Luisa and Mena are sisters-in-law; one extrovert and the other shy, they are united in friendship by the loss of a beloved husband and brother. They live just outside Rome, where huge umbrella pines sigh with distant sea breezes and in their local market you will find four or five varieties of artichoke for sale in the smallest of vegetable stalls.

Artichokes look a bit daunting to prepare but they are not, as long as you expect at least 50 per cent wastage. They are the culinary equivalent of jumping into a cold pool: don't mess about on the edge thinking if you ease yourself in gradually it will be okay. No, plunge in with a small paring knife and strip those spiky leaves from the base with a be firm-with-yourself frame of mind. They discolour quickly when cut, and Maria Luisa says you should keep a cut lemon to hand to smear over the surfaces as you prepare them – and before you plop them into some lemony water.

FOR THE PASTA
400 g (14 oz/3⅓ cups) 00 flour or plain (all-purpose) flour
4 eggs
1 tablespoon extra-virgin olive oil (optional)

FOR THE SAUCE
1.5 kg (3 lb 5 oz) artichokes, which when peeled and sliced gives you about 700 g (1 lb 9 oz)
7 lemons, sliced
200 g (7 oz) guanciale or pancetta
50 g (2 oz) grated Pecorino
salt

Make the pasta dough as described on page 18, adding the oil with the eggs if you like (for extra flavour). While it rests, make the sauce.

To prepare the artichokes, snap off all the tough outer leaves from the artichoke base until you reach the more tender yellow or leaf-green inner ones. Feel the artichoke head to find the point, moving from the base to the tips, where it ceases to be firm. Chop the tops off along this line. It's usually about a third of the leaves. Take a teaspoon and scoop out the hairy chokes. Take a cut lemon and rub the artichoke with lemon juice, then plop it into a bowl of water into which you've squeezed the juice of another lemon. Once you have prepped them all, the next step is to slice them as thinly as possible, returning the pieces to the lemon water.

When you are ready to cook the artichokes, drain the slices and place them in a sauté pan with a little water and season. Cover with the lid and let them simmer for 10–15 minutes, until the leaves are soft.

Meanwhile, dice your guanciale or pancetta so each bit has both meat and fat. Fry the pieces in a large non-stick frying pan (skillet), no oil needed, so the fat is released and the meat crisps a bit.

Roll out your sfoglia so it's about 2 mm thick, then roll it up like a carpet and cut across the pasta to create folded-over ribbons about 8 mm (½ in) wide. Shake them out and keep them well floured.

Place half of the cooked artichokes in a food processor and blitz them to a chunky purée. Return them to the pan with the rest of the artichokes and add the guanciale or pancetta and its fat (aim for a tablespoon or so – any more, spoon it off). Let this pan sit over a gentle heat while you cook the pasta.

Bring a large pan of salted water to the boil and add the pasta. Cook for about 2 minutes. Ladle out a spoonful of pasta water and add this to the artichokes, drain the pasta and toss it through the artichoke mixture along with some of the Pecorino. Plate up and sprinkle over the rest of the cheese.

Fettuccine – which means little ribbons in Italian – are the beloved pasta of Rome, and you'll find these ribbons made across the centre and south of Italy. Tagliatelle are from Emilia Romagna and Le Marche. Fettuccine are supposed to be a millimetre or so narrower and not as thinly rolled, but when it comes to homemade pasta, who is going to get out the ruler? The two can be used interchangeably in recipes.

GIUSEPPINA'S PICI WITH GARLIC TOMATO SAUCE

FOR 4 PEOPLE

Giuseppina Spiganti is 93 years old. She is something of a local treasure, as she is the last surviving member of the group which began a *pici sagra*, a local food festival, 50 years ago. The village of Celle sul Rigo had a marching band, which was in need of money, so a sagra, celebrating the local pasta, pici, was born. At the time it was very unusual to honour a poor dish; nowadays, the festival is so popular, the organisers need 800 kg (more than three-quarters of a ton) of flour to make enough pici for the crowds. The townspeople are fiercely proud of this tradition. Giuseppina was taught to make pici by her mother-in-law. One hundred kiliometres (60 miles) away, pici have turned into umbricelli. The dough loses the egg entirely and the shape becomes more uneven; umbricelli means 'looking like earthworms'. On the next page is Luciana's version.

FOR THE PASTA
400 g (14 oz/3⅓ cups) 00 flour
  or plain (all-purpose) flour
pinch of salt
1 egg
about 165 ml (5½ fl/⅔ cup) water
semolina flour, to roll the pici in

FOR THE GARLIC SAUCE
4 tablespoons extra-virgin olive oil
5 garlic cloves, ones that have not
  developed their 'anima' or green
  shoots
fresh red chilli peppers, to taste
  (Giuseppina used one, sliced
  into three)
2 tablespoons tomato purée
400 g (14 oz) plum tomatoes, preferably
  San Marzano
salt

The sauce has to simmer for a couple of hours, so start this before your pasta. Pour the olive oil into a small saucepan – it should cover the base to a depth of 5 mm (¼ in). Warm up the oil over a low heat and sauté the whole garlic cloves until you can crush them with a spoon; they shouldn't burn. This will take about 20 minutes. About 15 minutes into the cooking, add the chilli pepper, and continue frying the two ingredients for the final 5 minutes. Stir through the tomato purée, followed by the plum tomatoes. Break up the tomatoes with a wooden spoon, season with

salt, and add half a tin of water. Let this simmer very gently over a low heat for 2 hours, adding a splash of water from time to time if you need to. You want a thick sauce at the end. Giuseppina uses a food mill to purée the sauce – to make sure the garlic and chilli disappear. You could also use a hand-held blender.

Make the pasta dough as described on page 18 but swap 3 of the eggs for water. Fill a shallow bowl with semolina flour to drop your pici into, to stop them from sticking together. Place a small bowl of water to the side of your pasta board, so you can keep your fingers moist while rolling the dough into pici (or use a small spritzing bottle filled with water).

Roll the dough out quite thickly, about 5 mm (¼ in). Then slice it up, making 1 × 12 cm (½ × 5 in) batons. Take each one, place it on the board and place both your hands together over the pasta. Keep your fingers straight and roll out the pasta, moving your hands apart. You are creating a spaghetti strand, so try and keep the pasta even in thickness. Giuseppina's pici are much slimmer than some of the tubby versions you see on the Internet; aim for about 3 mm in diameter and 40 cm (15¾ in) long.

Drop your finished pici into the semolina. If the bowl starts getting a little crowded, move them onto a tray.

Bring a large pan of salted water to the boil and drop the pici in. Cook for 2 minutes and then test for doneness. Drain and stir through the sauce – you want it to cling to the pasta and not puddle around it. Serve immediately. Traditionally, no cheese is added.

LUCIANA'S UMBRICELLI WITH 'FAKE RAGÙ'

———

FOR 4 PEOPLE

Luciana Paolucci is a *contadina*, a farmer, in Umbria. She grows all her own food, from chickens to vegetables and wine to olive oil. She's a woman of charm and practicality. When her husband proposed, she asked for olive trees rather than a ring. And nothing is wasted in her kitchen; her chickens are her recycling units, as they get the scraps of pasta dough carefully scraped off the board after kneading.

Umbricelli are so called because they are meant to look like earthworms; uneven thickness is part of their charm – whereas Giuseppina (on page 75) prides herself on her slim, shoelace-style pici. The sauce or *sugo finto* (meaning fake ragù, as it's meatless) is a simple tomato sauce with garlic, parsley and cheese.

FOR THE PASTA

400 g (14 oz/3⅓ cups) soft wheat 0 flour or plain (all-purpose) flour
180–200 ml water (6–7 fl oz/ ¾–scant 1 cup) warm water
pinch of salt

FOR THE SUGO FINTO

2 garlic cloves, minced
3 tablespoons extra-virgin olive oil
a glass of white wine (about 175 ml/ 6 fl oz/¾ cup)
500 g (1 lb 2 oz) passata (sieved tomatoes) (Luciana makes her own)
pinch of salt
1 heaped tablespoon chopped parsley
50 g (2 oz) grated Pecorino or Parmigiano Reggiano

Luciana recommends making this pasta in a cool room because the dough dries out so easily. The absence of egg means this is a very soft dough – make it as described on page 21.

Keeping the dough covered, cut a walnut-sized piece off at a time and roll it out using flat palms, starting in the centre and working your way along the pasta rope. You can snip the length in two if it makes it easier to handle, but it's quite good fun to see how long you can make them. Cover them with a tea towel while you make the sugo finto.

Sauté the garlic in the olive oil and just as you think it's about to colour, pour in the wine – stand back as it bubbles. Let the alcohol boil off and then add the passata. Add a pinch of salt and let it simmer for 10 minutes. Stir in the chopped parsley.

While the sugo finto is cooking, bring a large saucepan of water to the boil, add a generous amount of salt and bring it back to the boil before adding the umbricelli. Stir and let them bob to the surface; they'll need about 2 minutes to cook. Drain them.

Marry the sauce and pasta in a serving bowl, along with the cheese and serve immediately.

It doesn't matter if the umbricelli are a bit irregular, but aim to make them roughly the same size so they cook evenly.

LAURA'S PIZZOCCHERI FROM VALTELLINA

FOR 6–8 HUNGRY PEOPLE
(quantities are easily halved)

The Valtellina is an area where the mountains rise, bruised purple with cold from the valley floor, while mist curtains cloak the upper slopes (we visited in mid-winter). It feels like Switzerland has strayed over the border with its dairy herds and wood-timbered alpine buildings. Here, you'll find *pizzoccheri*, a ribbon pasta made with buckwheat flour. Buckwheat only needs a short growing season and is suited to being farmed on high slopes. These days, production has mostly relocated to Poland, with local farmers now only growing enough for family use.

Pizzoccheri are traditionally served with potatoes, savoy cabbage, melted cheese and lots of garlicky butter. It's a dish to eat when you've had a day hiking or skiing. The Accademia del Pizzocchero di Teglio is an organisation dedicated to promoting this pasta, and they organise a food festival every year. Laura and Bianca from the Accademia showed us how it's made. Laura, in fact, comes from Milan and getting involved with pizzoccheri was a way for her to make friends while settling in to the village of Teglio. Bianca used to have her own restaurant.

The Accademia recommends using the local cheese Valtellina Casera DOP, which is tricky to find outside the area. Instead, you could also use fontina, Gruyère, Emmental or Bitto (also a local cheese). It will cease to be an authentic recipe, but don't let that stop you – it will still taste delicious.

FOR THE PASTA
400 g (14 oz/3⅓ cups) finely ground buckwheat flour
100 g (3½ oz) 00 flour or plain (all-purpose) flour
2 g (½ teaspoon) salt
about 250–300 ml (8½–10 fl oz/scant 1–1¼ cups) water (I found this varies quite a bit depending on the flour)

FOR THE SAUCE
200 g (7 oz) potato, peeled and cut into 3 cm (1½ in) dice
200 g (7 oz) savoy cabbage, roughly shredded
100 g (3½ oz) unsalted butter (reduce the quantity if you like)
2 garlic cloves, sliced
250 g (9 oz) Valtellina Casera DOP, shaved (to be authentic or see introduction for alternatives)
100 g (3½ oz) Parmigiano Reggiano or Grano Padano, grated

First make the pasta. Combine the flours and salt together and gradually mix in the water. You want a dough that feels smooth and plump, which neither crumbles nor sticks to your hands. It doesn't need to rest. Roll it out as you would pastry, to a thickness of about 2–3 mm. Then use a knife to make short tagliatelle, 7–8 cm (3 in) long and 5 mm (¼ in) wide.

To make the sauce, bring a large pot of salted water to the boil. Add the potatoes and let them cook for a couple of minutes before chucking in the cabbage. After another 5 minutes, add the pasta to the same pot and continue to cook everything for around 10 minutes, until the pizzoccheri are done – test one to check. Have ready a warmed baking dish or platter.

Melt the butter in a frying pan (skillet) and sauté the garlic until it is slightly golden but not burnt. Put it to one side while you assemble the pasta with the cheese: drain the pasta and potato-cabbage mixture, and add some to the warmed platter, followed by a scattering of both cheeses. Repeat the layers, finishing with the cheese. Warm up your garlic butter and pour it over everything. Do not mix it.

Some cooks finish the pasta off in a hot oven, so the cheese melts and bubbles.

ROSA'S 'STRAW' AND 'HAY' TAGLIATELLE WITH PEAS

FOR 6 PEOPLE

Rosa is a bustling, joyous, tiny woman who needs a step to reach her pasta board properly. Now retired, she worked as a machine-embroidery seamstress in a local clothing factory and still has a machine tucked away in the corner of her kitchen for those odd jobs people continue to ask her to do.

Making pasta for her is like doing the laundry: it's a task she is happy to do, and she takes great satisfaction in the end result. Rosa shrugged her shoulders and looked nonplussed when I asked her what the key to good pasta making was. 'Well, it's what you do, isn't it? You must have good flour, you must knead it properly,' she replied, as she vigorously continued to stretch out the dough. Rosa says, 'adding spinach makes pasta dough more fragile, so use the food processor to blend the spinach with the eggs to make a liquid'. This way the dough is more uniform.

This dish hails from Emilia Romagna, where mushrooms may be swapped for the peas in the autumn.

FOR THE 'STRAW' PASTA
300 g (10½ oz/2½ cups) 00 flour
   or plain (all-purpose) flour
3 eggs

FOR THE 'HAY' PASTA
300 g (10½ oz/2½ cups) 00 flour
   or plain (all-purpose) flour
2 eggs
100 g (3½ oz) fresh spinach

FOR THE PEA DRESSING
3 tablespoons extra-virgin olive oil
50 g (2 oz) unsmoked pancetta, cubed
1 large onion, finely sliced
200 g (7 oz) small peas (fresh or frozen,
   depending on the time of year)
250 g (9 oz) passata (sieved tomatoes)
salt

TO SERVE
grated Parmigiano Reggiano

Make the two types of pasta dough (straw and hay) as described on page 18. For the spinach dough, do as Rosa says and blend the spinach and eggs together before adding the mixture to the flour, then continue making the dough as normal. Roll out both pastas into large discs, about 2 mm thick. While the sfoglias rest, make the pea dressing.

Heat the olive oil in a sauté pan and add the pancetta. Fry it to release some of its fat, then add the sliced onion. Continue to sauté until the onion is soft, which will take around 7 minutes. Stir in the peas and passata and season with some salt. Add a cup of water and then let the sauce reduce until it is thick; so that when you push your spoon through it, you can see the base of the pan briefly.

Roll up the yellow sfoglia as you would a carpet and cut across the pasta to create folded over ribbons about 7 mm (¾ in) wide. Shake them out, then repeat with the spinach sfoglia. Rosa rolls up the sfoglia together, as shown in the photo but it's much easier to do them separately. Mix up the ribbons by tossing them together with your fingers.

Bring a large pan of salted water to the boil. Drop in the pasta ribbons and once the pan has returned to the boil, cook them for 2–3 minutes – test them for doneness.

Keeping back a couple of ladles of pasta water just in case you want to loosen the pea mixture, drain the tagliatelle, and toss it with the peas – you want the two colours to be evenly coated with the sauce. Serve with plenty of grated Parmigiano Reggiano.

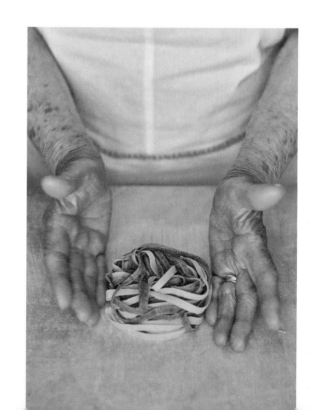

PINA'S CURZUL WITH SHALLOT SAUCE

FOR 4 PEOPLE

Curzul is a square-sided spaghetti found in the Faenza region of Emilia Romagna. In the local dialect, the name means shoestring or a priest's rope belt. It is popularly paired with a variety of shallot grown locally called *scalogno* – but you can use any that's available in your greengrocers.

Pina lives deep in the countryside, surrounded by hectares of kiwi orchards. She started making pasta when she was just 9 years old and that is about all I know about her, because she is amazingly shy! Note the small quantity of sausage meat used in this recipe; it's a shallot sauce and the sausage is there just for flavouring.

FOR THE PASTA
400 g (14 oz/3⅓ cups) 00 flour
    or plain (all-purpose) flour
4 eggs

FOR THE SHALLOT SAUCE
3 tablespoons extra-virgin olive oil
6 good-sized shallots, diced
    (about 500 g/1 lb 2 oz in total)
2 good-quality fresh Italian sausages
pinch of peperoncino
a glass of white wine (125 ml/4 fl oz/
    ½ cup)
300 g (10½ oz) passata (sieved
    tomatoes)
salt and pepper

Make the pasta dough as described on page 18. Roll it out to the thickness of ordinary shortcrust pastry – i.e. it doesn't have to be as see-through thin as regular tagliatelle. Aim for about 2–3 mm thick. Flour it well and roll it up like a carpet. Then using a very sharp knife, cut across the pasta to create folded over ribbons about 3 mm wide. Shake the ribbons out, and spread them out to dry a little.

Meanwhile, to make the sauce, heat the olive oil in a frying pan (skillet) over a medium heat and fry the diced shallots for several minutes until they are softened. Strip the sausages of their skins and crumble them into the pan. Continue frying the meat and shallots until the sausage meat is lightly browned. Stir in the peperoncino, add the wine to deglaze the pan, then let some of the alcohol cook off before adding the passata. Reduce the heat, and let everything simmer for 20 minutes or until the sauce is thick. Check for seasoning halfway through: Italian sausages are often quite salty, so you may not need to add any extra.

Bring a large pan of water to the boil, add a generous pinch of salt, bring it back to the boil and add the pasta. Cook for a couple of minutes and nibble a strand to test for doneness. Drain, mix with the sauce, and eat immediately.

In Faenza, they don't serve the dish with any Parmigiano Reggiano, as they like to taste the shallots. The pasta police won't come knocking on your door if you do, though!

MARICA'S STRAPPONI WITH PORCINI MUSHROOMS

FOR 4 PEOPLE

The Garfagnana region of Tuscany is steeply wooded and rural – quite different from the more well-known parts of the area. Not only is the area a mushroom-hunter's heaven, the mint the Italians call *nepitella* (*Calamintha nepeta*) grows wild here, too. So, this is a forager's supper, and it is also an ace pasta for beginners. *Strapponi* are hand-torn pieces of pasta, ripped any which way; these ragged bits of pasta are also called *straccetti*.

Marica demonstrated this for us. She is a cook at the Agriturismo Venturo, in a little town called Castelnuovo where we stayed during filming in the region. She's too young to be a nonna but her recipe is too good to pass over! If you can only find dried porcini mushrooms, then use fresh mushrooms of a different variety – mixed wild mushroom, girolles or chanterelle will also work.

FOR THE PASTA
400 g (14 oz/3⅓ cups) 00 flour
    or plain (all-purpose) flour
4 eggs

FOR THE DRESSING
4 tablespoons extra-virgin olive oil
2 garlic cloves
3 tablespoons chopped fresh mint
    (preferably nepitella)
500 g (1 lb 2 oz) fresh porcini
    mushrooms, chopped (see
    introduction for alternatives)
salt

Make the pasta dough as described on page 18. Once it has rested for 30 minutes, roll it out to the thickness of ordinary shortcrust pastry – i.e. it doesn't have to be as see-through thin as tagliatelle. Aim for about 2–3 mm thick. Roll it up around your pin while you make the sauce.

To make the dressing, heat the olive oil in a large sauté pan. Add the garlic and mint and fry the mixture for a couple of minutes, before adding the chopped mushrooms. Keep frying to soften the mushrooms, season them with a pinch of salt, and add 100 ml (3½ fl oz/scant ½ cup) of water. Let this cook off, then continue frying the mushrooms until they are golden. Remove the garlic.

Bring a large saucepan of water to the boil, salt it, and return it to the boil. Keeping the pasta rolled around your rolling pin, hold the pin above and near the water (don't burn yourself in the steam) and pull pieces off and drop them in the water. This is how Marica does it. For those of you who don't want to brandish your rolling pin, simply tear off pasta strips/ squares/odd shapes roughly the size of a credit card and then dump them in the boiling water. Cook for 2–3 minutes, depending on the thickness of your pasta pieces.

Drain and add the pasta to the mushroom mixture. Give everything a good stir and toss together. And you're done; the pasta is ready. In Garfagnana, this is not served with cheese.

three

Pulses

Every region of Italy has a recipe
for pasta served with a pulse of
some kind. These everyday dishes
are heart-warming, just like the
cooks who make them.

ADA'S TAGLIOLI AND BEAN SOUP

FOR 6 PEOPLE

Ada's recipe is actually a soup. These *tagliolini* are stubby, not the long ribbons you find elsewhere in Italy. It's a good example of the same name being given to a different-shaped pasta, as you so often find across the country. Sugo finto means 'a sauce without meat', but Ada likes to make a semi-sugo finto sauce, as she fries pancetta with a little garlic, and adds the fat along with the beans. Ortavio, Ada's husband, then has the pancetta for his *secondo* (main course). Ada's other secret ingredient is powdered rosemary. She dries twigs of rosemary in the sun until they're snappy and crisp, then strips the leaves and blitzes them in a spice blender; no more needles!

FOR THE PASTA

300 g (10½ oz/scant 2½ cups) 00 flour
    or plain (all-purpose) flour
1 egg, beaten
90 ml (3 fl oz) water

FOR THE SUGO FINTO

150 g (5 oz) dried borlotti (cranberry)
    beans or 300 g (10 oz) cooked beans
2 tablespoons extra-virgin olive oil
1 onion, finely chopped
1 carrot, finely diced
400 g (14 oz) passata (sieved tomatoes)
3 bay leaves
1 tablespoon powdered rosemary leaves
    (see introduction)
2 thick-cut rashers of unsmoked pancetta
    (optional)
1 garlic clove (optional)
salt

TO SERVE

grated Parmigiano Reggiano (optional)

If you are using dried borlotti beans, place them in a bowl and cover with enough water to submerge them by several centimetres (at least a couple of inches). Add a teaspoon of salt and leave them for at least 8 hours, or ideally overnight. Drain them of their soaking water, place them in a pan with fresh water and simmer them until cooked. How long the beans take to cook will depend on their freshness, but it will be around 45 minutes–1 hour. Drain and set aside.

Tip the flour onto your pasta board in a heap. Make a well and add the beaten egg. Use a fork to mix the flour gradually into the egg, followed by half the water. Start forming it into a dough and if it feels a bit dry, add a little more water. You want to end up with a firm dough that holds together easily but is not sticky. Knead for 10 minutes. Cover it with a tea towel (or put it in a lidded bowl) and leave it for 30 minutes.

On a floured work surface, roll out the dough to a thickness of about 2 mm. You now want to make short ribbons of pasta around 10 cm (4 in) long and 5 mm (¼ in) wide – it doesn't have be exactly this, just be consistent so they will take the same amount of time to cook. Ada has a good trick to speed up the process: roll the dough around your pin, take a knife and slice lengthways along the pin to create wide strips of pasta. If these pasta lengths are too wide, slice them again in half lengthways. Then assemble the lengths one on top of the other. Slice across them at 5 mm (¼ in) intervals to create short ribbons.

Let the pasta rest while you make the sugo finto. Heat the olive oil in a sauté pan and fry the onion and carrot over a medium heat until they are soft but not caramelised. Add the passata, bay leaves, rosemary and beans. Season with salt and give everything a good stir, then reduce the heat and leave to simmer for 10 minutes.

If using pancetta, sauté it in a small pan over a medium heat along with the whole garlic clove, long enough for the fat to be released. Remove the garlic and pour the fat into the beans. You can keep it to one side to sprinkle over the final dish.

Bring a large saucepan of salted water to the boil, then add the pasta. Cook for 2 minutes – test for doneness – then remove about half to two-thirds of the water (depending on how chunky or thin you like your soup). Add the bean mixture, stir it through the pasta and sprinkle over cheese (if desired).

CESARINA'S PIACENZA-STYLE PASTA AND BEANS

—

FOR 6 PEOPLE

Pisarei are northern Italy's equivalent of cavatelli (see page 92). They are the same shape, but made with a completely different dough. It is a typical pasta from the city of Piacenza and the surrounding area.

Cesarina bubbled with enthusiasm when she shared her recipe with me. 'Ooh I'm a *buongustaia* (a gourmet)! I learned to make pasta when I got married at 17.' She improved her skills while working as a household help when she was younger, and often cooks just for herself because she says her husband isn't interested in food.

'The key to a really good plate of *pisarei e fasò* is, first, to use stock in the dough. Some recipes say water or milk, but the flavour is so much better when you use a nice meat stock. Secondly, try and make the pisarei as small as possible.'

FOR THE PASTA
400 g (14 oz/3⅓ cups) 00 flour
    or plain (all-purpose) flour
100 g (3½ oz) fine breadcrumbs
about 200 ml (7 fl oz/scant 1 cup)
    warm meat stock (see page 203)

FOR THE FASÒ
175 g (6 oz) dried borlotti (cranberry)
    beans
75 g (2½ oz) lardo or fatty pancetta
2 sprigs of rosemary, leaves stripped
1 onion, chopped
pinch of ground nutmeg
pinch of ground cloves
pinch of pepper
1 bay leaf
handful of chopped parsley
300 g (10½ oz) passata (sieved
    tomatoes)
salt

TO SERVE
grated Parmigiano Reggiano

Place the beans in a bowl and cover with enough water to submerge them. Add a pinch of salt and soak them for 8 hours, or ideally overnight.

Drain the beans and put them in a saucepan. Pour in enough cold water to cover the beans by about 10 cm (4 in). Bring to a simmer and cook until the beans are soft, adding a little water if needed. How long this takes will depend on your beans, but it will be around 45 minutes–1 hour. You will be left with 350 g (12 oz) cooked weight of beans. Drain and set aside.

To make the pasta, mix the flour and breadcrumbs together and heap into a pile. Make a well in the middle, then add the stock a little at a time, incorporating it fully before adding any more. Keep kneading until the dough starts feeling silky to touch. Transfer to a bowl and cover with a tea towel (or use a lidded bowl) and leave it for 30 minutes to relax.

Take a handful of dough and roll it into a thin rope about 1 cm (½ in) in diameter. Pinch a pea-sized piece off the end and roll it along the pasta board, pressing hard with your thumb to create a curved shape. Repeat until you've used all of the dough, keeping the pieces of pasta under a tea towel to stop them from drying out while you make the sauce.

Using a sharp knife, mince the lardo or pancetta with the rosemary to form a paste (this is known as *pistà 'd grass*). Melt this in a large sauté pan over a medium heat and then add the onion and fry until soft. Add all the other ingredients, including the cooked beans, and simmer for a good 15 minutes or so for the flavours to get to know each other.

Bring a large pot of salted water to the boil then add the pasta. The pisarei will float to the surface when cooked. Scoop them out with a slotted spoon or sieve and add to the bean mixture. Stir together along with some cheese and serve.

CARMELA'S CAVATELLI RIGATI WITH BEANS FROM LECCE

FOR 4-6 PEOPLE

Carmela and her family have a small farm just beyond the Lecce ring road. If you asked a child to describe a farm, Carmela's would tick most of the boxes: it has dogs and horses, cows and doves, sturdy rows of vegetables and swallows swooping through it all. Carmela says, 'Growing up, when the family came round, we had to eat outside because there were about 60 of us. Everyone would bring a dish. Nowadays the family is smaller, and I only cook for 12 on Sundays. This dish is a good way to feed lots of people.'

To make this dish richer, Carmela suggests folding a tin of drained ventresca tuna through the beans and pasta at the end instead of the speck. 'This was a special treat as a child – meat was too expensive for my family.' You probably haven't been able to grow your own cannellini beans like Carmela, but it's worth cooking the beans yourself rather than resorting to a tin.

FOR THE PASTA
400 g (14 oz/3⅓ cups) semolina flour
180–200 ml (6–7 fl oz/¾–1 cup)
    warm water

FOR THE BEANS
200 g (7 oz) dried cannellini beans
1 onions, quartered
2 ripe tomatoes, chopped
a handful of parsley, leaves and stalks,
    roughly chopped
salt

FOR THE SAUCE
2 tablespoons extra-virgin olive oil
1 onion, sliced
2 thick rashers of speck or smoked
    pancetta, sliced into nuggets
extra-virgin olive oil, to drizzle

Place the beans in a bowl and cover with enough water to submerge them by several centimetres (at least a couple of inches). Add a teaspoon of salt and soak them for 8 hours, or ideally overnight.

Meanwhile, make the pasta dough as described on page 21 and allow to rest.

Drain the beans and put them in a saucepan with the quartered onion, tomatoes and parsley. Pour in enough cold water to cover the beans by about 10 cm (4 in). Bring to a simmer and cook until the beans are soft, adding a little water if needed. How long this takes will depend on your beans, but it will be around 45 minutes–1 hour. You will be left with 400 g (14 oz) cooked weight of beans.

While the beans are cooking, make the *cavatelli rigati* (the pasta). Take a handful of dough, keeping the rest covered with a tea towel. Roll out the dough into a rope about the thickness of a wooden spoon handle. Slice it into squarish pillows, then roll each piece along a cavatelli board (if you have one) or the back of a fork, pushing down with your thumb. Your cavatelli will be about the same size as your cooked beans. Keep them spread out on a tray or board. Repeat until you have used all the dough.

When ready to cook, heat the oil in a large frying pan (skillet) and sauté the onion and pancetta for about 7 minutes, until the onion is soft. Scoop the beans from their cooking water with a sieve or slotted spoon and add them to the frying pan. Bring some salted water to the boil in a separate large saucepan then add the pasta. The cavatelli should bob to the surface when cooked – but test one after a couple of minutes.

Drain the pasta (use the bean cooking water to create more of a sauce if necessary) and add it to the beans. Mix together and serve with a drizzle of oil.

ANNA'S CRESC'TAJAT WITH BEANS

FOR 6 PEOPLE

Anna lives in a converted watermill, now her B&B, where silk-makers used to come and wash their material. We visited her when the building was wreathed in wisteria flowers and with the background sounds of rushing water over pebbles and the shouts of paddling holiday makers enjoying National Liberation Day. Anna is a keen cook who enjoys sharing the traditional recipes of the Pesaro and Urbino area with her guests. *Cresc'tajat* (pronounced *cresh-tie-et*) is a fine example of frugal cooking. It used to be made with leftover polenta (cornmeal) and served with stewed wild greens or beans, which is what Anna made for us.

Lardo is cured pork fat; if you can't find it in an Italian deli, then use pancetta or mince up some unsmoked streaky bacon instead.

FOR THE PASTA
200 g (7 oz) instant polenta (cornmeal)
100 g (3½ oz) 00 flour or plain (all-purpose) flour

FOR THE BEANS
250 g (9 oz) dried borlotti (cranberry) beans
1 carrot
1 celery stick
50 g (2 oz) lardo or fatty pancetta
4 tablespoons extra-virgin olive oil
1 onion, sliced
1 garlic clove, minced
1 meaty, top-quality fresh sausage, skin removed (but not discarded) and crumbled
200 g (7 oz) passata (sieved tomatoes)
salt

TO SERVE
50 g (2 oz) grated Pecorino
extra-virgin olive oil

The day before you want to serve this dish, make the polenta according to the packet instructions. The polenta will stiffen up as it cools and, before using it, it should be cold and firm, but you should still be able to cut it with a fork. You want about 300 g (10 oz) cooked weight.

Soak the beans for 8 hours or overnight – place them in a bowl and cover with enough water to submerge them by several centimetres (at least a couple of inches). Drain them and then simmer in a pan of water with the carrot and celery (this helps to flavour the broth) until the beans are cooked

through. How long they take to cook will depend on the freshness of your beans, but it will be around 45 minutes–1 hour. Keep them in their broth to one side while you make the pasta.

Mash the cooked polenta with the flour and then knead until smooth and you cannot see any streaks of flour. Divide the dough into 3 pieces and shape each piece into a patty. Keeping them well floured, roll them out as you would pastry – aim for about 2-3 mm thick. Slice into broad strips (about 4 cm/ 1½ in wide), then cut along the strips on the diagonal to create small diamond shapes.

To prevent the pasta sticking together, Anna places the pieces in a single layer on a tray and pops them into the freezer until ready to cook.

Mince the lardo or pancetta by chopping it with a mezzaluna or a sharp, heavy knife. Heat it with the oil over a moderate heat and fry the onion until soft, which will take about 7 minutes. Add the garlic and cook for a further minute. Fry the sausage meat in the onion mixture until browned, which will take another 5 minutes or so, and then pour in the passata along with a couple of ladles of the bean broth. Season with salt and leave everything to simmer for a good 15 minutes. If you like, you can put the pork skin in at this stage to add some extra flavour.

Strain the beans and add these to the tomato sauce to warm through.

Bring a large saucepan of water to the boil, add some salt, and return the water to the boil. Take your cresc'tajat from the freezer and tip them directly into the water. When they bob to the surface, they are ready. Using a sieve or slotted spoon, scoop the pasta from the water and stir it through the bean mixture.

Serve immediately and let everyone sprinkle their own plates with cheese and drizzle with oil.

EUGENIA'S FREGULA AND BEAN SOUP

FOR 4 PEOPLE

Eugenia lives in Montresta, a tiny village in north-west Sardinia. Her house has mountain views. You approach her home through a happy mix of flowers and herbs, and it takes a moment to notice she has a second kitchen to the side of one terrace. It looks like a garden shed, but inside it has a special kind of pasta beater only found in Sardinia, a freezer and all sorts of bottling equipment. It's a secret cave for keen cooks.

Fregula is Sardinian for fregola – the name used to describe little balls of pasta, which can be toasted. Eugenia says, 'Fregula was invented to give texture and interest to pulses and vegetables.' While most people these days buy their fregula, Eugenia magics hers into existence in less than an hour. The method is the same process as for making couscous and you will need the more coarsely ground, sandy-textured semolina.

One of the many other things Eugenia makes herself are intensely savoury sun-dried tomatoes. She slices plum-shaped tomatoes in half, sprinkles the cut surfaces with a little coarse salt, and leaves them in a huge, flat, reed basket to dry in the sun. She then covers each half with a basil leaf and freezes them until needed. Her tomatoes are sweet, not too salty and an instant pick-me-up for all kinds of dishes.

FOR THE PASTA
1 teaspoon salt
250 ml (8 fl oz/1 cup) tepid water
300 g (10½ oz/scant 2½ cups) coarsely
    ground semolina flour

FOR THE SOUP
250 g (9 oz) dried chickpeas (garbanzo
    beans)
1 onion, sliced
a handful of wild fennel fronds, chopped
4 good-quality sun-dried tomatoes,
    chopped
extra-virgin olive oil, to drizzle

Place the chickpeas in a bowl and cover with enough water to submerge them by several centimetres (at least a couple of inches). Soak them for 8 hours, or ideally overnight. Then drain them.

To make the pasta, dissolve the salt in the water in a small bowl. Splash a bit into a large mixing bowl (Eugenia uses a flat-bottomed earthenware dish with a diameter of about 40 cm/15¾ in), followed by a couple of tablespoons of the semolina.

Using the tips of your fingers, stir the flour into the water using a circular motion. Little balls of dough will begin to form. Alternate adding more water and flour, making sure there is never too much of either. You will start to create fregula of varying sizes, but ideally they should be about the same size as a small chickpea. Remove them as you go along and spread them on a tray to dry out. Keep going until you have used all the flour. Divide your pasta into large and small fregula, by shaking your tray – the large ones will rise to the surface.

Put the chickpeas, onion, fennel fronds and sun-dried tomatoes in a large saucepan. Cover with enough water to submerge the contents by about 10 cm (4 in). Simmer until the chickpeas are soft, which will take about 1 hour. Once they are cooked, add all except the very smallest fregula (which can be used as the starter for your next batch) and simmer for a couple of minutes to cook through.

Ladle into bowls, and serve with a drizzle of extra-virgin olive oil. Heaven.

MARIA AND ROSARIA'S CHICKPEA AND PASTA SOUP

———

FOR 4-6 PEOPLE

Ciceri e tria is a classic dish from the Salento region of Puglia, in the heel of Italy. It is a pottage of tagliatelle and chickpeas (garbanzo beans), given a scattering of fried, crunchy pasta as you serve it. The local name for this dish is *massa*, which means thick soup. Traditionally, it was a Lent dish, given to the poor on St Joseph's day, 19 March, in the run up to Easter, and dating back to the time when the Arabs ruled Puglia during the 9th century.

Ninety-four-year-old Maria and Rosaria are friends through a prayer group, which meets every evening in the village of Torrepaduli. Maria needs a little bit of help in the kitchen, so Rosaria was with her when we filmed the making of this recipe in the village's agricultural museum, the Museo della Civiltá Contadina.

Rosaria used the open range to cook the chickpeas in a *pignata*, an earthenware amphora-shaped vessel. She added soaked chickpeas to the pot with some water and placed it directly among the hot embers. When they came to the boil, she scooped off the foam and added a sliced onion. She then left them to cook for another hour or two, resulting in lovely creamy chickpeas. If you don't have an open fire or an earthenware cooking pot, then cook as described below.

FOR THE PASTA
400 g (14 oz/3⅓ cups) semolina flour
180-200 ml (6-7 fl oz/¾-1 cup) water

FOR THE MASSA
200 g (7 oz) dried chickpeas (garbanzo beans)
1 teaspoon salt
2 onions, sliced
vegetable oil, for frying
salt

Place the chickpeas in a bowl and cover with enough water to submerge them by several centimetres (at least a couple of inches). Add a teaspoon of salt and leave them for at least 8 hours, or ideally overnight.

Drain the chickpeas, place them in a saucepan with plenty of cold water and bring to the boil. Skim off the froth and add one of the sliced onions. Continue cooking until the chickpeas are tender to the bite – how long this takes will depend on your chickpeas, so keep checking them. It will take about 1 hour.

While your chickpeas are cooking, make the pasta dough as described on page 21.

After resting the dough, roll out a sfoglia to a thickness of about 2 mm, then roll it up like a carpet and cut across the pasta to create folded over ribbons about 1 cm (½ in) wide. Shake out the ribbons, keeping them well floured and spread out.

Ten minutes before you want to eat, pour vegetable oil into a large deep-sided pan to a depth of about 5 mm (¼ in). You are going to fry a quarter of your pasta, so if your pan is on the small side, you may have to fry it in batches. Heat the oil until it shimmers but isn't smoking. Add the pasta and fry them until they are crisp and golden. Use a slotted spoon or sieve to remove the ribbons and transfer them to a plate lined with kitchen paper.

Once you have fried the pasta, add the remaining onion to the pan and fry in the oil until soft. Add the cooked chickpeas and most of their cooking water – use your judgement at this point, you want enough water to cook the pasta in, but you don't want a thin watery soup at the end. Season with salt and bring everything to a simmer. Add the remaining raw pasta. It will only take few minutes to cook, so check on it – tasting one for doneness.

To serve, ladle the massa into bowls and scatter over the fried pasta. Eat immediately.

LETIZIA'S TAGLIATELLE WITH PURÉED DRIED BROAD BEANS

FOR 6 PEOPLE

Letizia wrote me a little essay on pasta to make sure we didn't forget anything. At 100 years old, she may need a zimmer frame, but she is mentally as sharp as a tack. I asked her what the secret is to healthy longevity, and she says one has to stay busy – and to find your inner strength when terrible things happen. She was thinking of the recent death of her daughter.

Practising what she believes, Letizia continues to write poems and loves to paint. She was a primary school teacher all her working life and has lived in her family's summer house ever since the big earthquake in Sicily in 1968 destroyed her original home. (Italians often have a second home in the countryside, not far from their main one in town.)

Her dish of tagliatelle with a dried broad (fava) bean purée and wild fennel is humble but delicious. Wild fennel doesn't have a bulb, but a tenacious root. Sow some seeds in the sunniest spot in your garden and you'll have fresh fennel fronds forevermore.

FOR THE PASTA
600 g (1 lb 7 oz/3½ cups) semolina flour,
    preferably a heritage wheat variety
300 ml (10 fl oz/1¼ cups)
    tepid water
1 g (¼ teaspoon) salt

FOR THE BEANS
4 tablespoons extra-virgin olive oil
1 onion, finely diced
1 carrot, finely diced
400 g (14 oz) dried, ready shelled broad
    (fava) beans
small bunch of wild fennel (use a pinch
    of crushed fennel seeds if you can't
    find wild fennel)
1 bay leaf
salt

TO SERVE
extra-virgin olive oil, to drizzle
½ teaspoon crushed dried chilli
    (optional)
fresh fennel fronds (optional)

Make the pasta dough as described on page 21. Roll the dough out to a thickness of about 2 mm, then use a knife to cut 3 mm wide ribbons.

Pour olive oil into a non-stick saucepan and warm it up over medium heat before adding the onion and carrot. (If you don't have wild fennel, add the crushed fennel seeds now.) Sauté the vegetables until they have softened, which will take 7–10 minutes. Add the broad beans and cover with plenty of water. Drop in some wild fennel fronds and the bay leaf and let the mixture simmer until the beans start to collapse; how long this will take will depend on the beans, but you should estimate at least 20 minutes for this stage. Add more water if necessary but remember you are aiming for a thick purée. Do not wander off – beans have a tendency to stick to the bottom of the pan if you don't stir them regularly.

Remove the bay leaf and season the bean purée with salt, to taste. Chop up some more fennel fronds and stir through the mixture.

Bring a large pan of salted water to the boil and drop in the pasta. The pasta will take about 5 minutes to cook. Nibble one to check for doneness.

Add a ladleful of pasta water to the bean purée. Drain the pasta and toss it with the beans. Ladle it into bowls, drizzle olive oil over each serving, and a scattering of chilli, if people would like it and more fennel fronds (if using).

GIOVANNA'S TAGLIOLINI AND RED BEAN SOUP

———

FOR 4 PEOPLE

Tuscans love their beans, and there is a wonderful array of varieties that are only grown in Tuscany. A good illustration of this is a little shop in the backstreets of Lucca, which is an Aladdin's cave of pulses: plump sacks jostling and clacking, full of beans with fabulous names like *piattellini* (little plates), *burrino* (a shade of yellow) and *diavolino* (little devil).

We visited Giovanna on a day when her husband was ill in bed, but she still managed a smile and to give us a generous welcome. This *taglioni sui fagioli* soup is her standard winter dish and she uses a red bean called *rosso di Lucca*, grown by her cousin Giovanni. It's a little bit smaller than a kidney bean and its flavour is savoury, almost meaty. Try and get hold of some if you can, or at least cook some dried beans rather than reaching for a tin – the result will be much more flavoursome. Giovanna says, 'Keep tasting! You don't want the beans to be bland!'

FOR THE PASTA
300 g (10½ oz/scant 2½ cups) stoneground wholemeal flour
2 tablespoons extra-virgin olive oil
135–150 ml (4–5 fl oz/½–⅔ cup) warm water

FOR THE BEAN SOUP
250 g (9 oz) dried red beans, such as rosso di Lucca or borlotti (cranberry)
1 large garlic clove
3 sage leaves
4 tablespoons extra-virgin olive oil
1 onion, sliced
1 large carrot, sliced
1 celery stick, sliced
2 tablespoons tomato purée
salt and pepper

TO SERVE
a peppery-tasting Tuscan extra-virgin olive oil

Place the beans in a bowl and cover with enough water to submerge them by several centimetres (at least a couple of inches). Leave them to soak for 8 hours, or ideally overnight. Drain them of their soaking water and put them in a saucepan with the garlic clove and sage leaves. Pour in enough water to submerge the beans to a depth of about 10 cm (4 in). Bring to a simmer and cook until the beans have no chalky centre. This will take a good hour, probably more. Top up the water during the cooking process, as needed.

When the beans are cooked, discard the garlic and sage. Keeping the water, drain the beans and set to one side while you make the pasta.

Make the pasta dough as described on page 21. While the pasta rests, in a large saucepan, heat the oil then sauté the onion, carrot and celery for 5 minutes until starting to soften. Stir in the tomato purée, and then ladle in some of the bean water to cover the vegetables. Simmer until soft, then mix in the cooked beans.

Blitz with a hand-held blender, adding more bean water if necessary. It should be soupily stirrable. Adjust the seasoning with salt and pepper, to taste. Keep the mixture warm while you make the pasta, but do watch out as puréed beans can catch and burn on the bottom of the pan very easily.

Roll out the pasta as you would shortcrust pastry – this flour won't allow you to go ultra-thin; aim for about 2–3 mm thick. Give the surface a light dusting of flour. Roll up the pasta sheet like a carpet, then cut across it to create folded over 1 cm (½ in) wide 'tagliolini' ribbons.

Add the pasta to the bean purée and let everything simmer gently, stirring regularly. Pasta takes longer to cook this way, so keep checking and expect it to take around 10 minutes.

Spoon into bowls and serve with a drizzle of peppery-tasting Tuscan extra-virgin olive oil.

LUIGIA'S MANATE WITH CHICKPEAS

FOR 6 PEOPLE

Manate is a ribbon pasta, found in the Castelmezzano area of Basilicata. It uses a very interesting method to make it, which doesn't involve rolling out a sfoglia first. Its name changes depending on where you are in southern Italy – down the road in the village of Ginestra it's called *dors* in the local dialect.

Luigia has a ready laugh and wasn't at all fazed being filmed in a local restaurant. She says, 'I was part of a large family and we had to make pasta – we couldn't afford to buy it.' Squeezing and stretching the dough, she created a kind of short tagliatelle, which she then served with a simple chickpea (garbanzo beans) and tomato *condimento*. 'This is a typical way to serve this pasta,' she says.

FOR THE PASTA

400 g (14 oz/3⅓ cups) semolina flour
pinch of salt
180–200 ml (6–7 fl oz/¾–1 cup) water

FOR THE CHICKPEA AND TOMATO SAUCE

3–4 tablespoons extra-virgin olive oil
1 onion, chopped
300 g (10 ½ oz) cooked tin or jarred
    chickpeas (garbanzo beans) (see how
    to cook dried chickpeas on page 100)
300 g (10 ½ oz) passata (sieved
    tomatoes)
1 teaspoon salt
handful of fresh basil leaves
extra-virgin olive oil, to drizzle

Make the pasta dough according to the instructions on page 21. The easiest way to describe how to make manata ribbons is to refer you to Luigia's video on the Pasta Grannies channel on YouTube. But if you don't have access to the Internet, here goes . . .

Once your dough has rested, press it into a slipper shape. You want to make a ring of pasta: use a sharp knife to slice down the middle to create a horizontal slit all the way through the dough. Using the palms of your hands, gently widen the slit and rotate the dough round, shaping it into a ring. Keep rolling and working the dough around the circle, to increase its circumference and thin out the dough. Keep going until you have a smooth rope which is about 1 cm

(½ in) in diameter. Then, channelling your childhood rodeo cowboy dreams, loosely loop the rope around one hand about 6 times.

Hold the coiled rope in both hands, palms up. Decide which is your squeezing hand and place that in front of what is now your pulling hand. Use your pulling hand to stretch the pasta towards your body, feeding it through the hand in front, which squeezes it as it passes through. Make sure to keep your pasta ropes well floured.

The strands will increase in length and once they are long enough, you can loop them over your hand again a few times and repeat the process. Stop when the ribbons resemble tagliatelle. (In Abruzzo, by the way, this process results in a pasta called *maccheroni alla mugnaia*, which stays as one long loop.) Slice the ribbons into 10 cm (4 in) lengths. Leave them spread out on the board or tray to dry a little.

To make the chickpea and tomato sauce, heat the oil in a saucepan over a medium heat and sauté the onion until it is soft; this will take a good 5 minutes. Add the chickpeas, passata, salt and basil leaves and give everything a good stir. Leave the sauce to simmer for 10 minutes, until it has thickened slightly.

Bring a large saucepan of water to the boil, add some salt and return to the boil. Throw the pasta ribbons in and cook for a few minutes – check one to make sure it's cooked. Drain and add the pasta to the chickpeas. Drizzle a little extra-virgin olive oil over everything before serving.

four

Potato and gnocchi

Gnocchi are found all over Italy, with variations in the shape and ingredients. They are one of the original forms of pasta and probably spent several centuries undocumented, but the first mention of them is in a 14th century manuscript. They were a way of using up leftover ingredients – just as ravioli are – and a testament to the ingenuity of frugal cooks!

DOMENICA'S RAVIOLE DI VALLE VARAITA

———

FOR 4 PEOPLE

Raviole are not ravioli but cigar-shaped gnocchi made in the Varaita valley, close to the French border in Piemonte. The potato is mixed with a local cow's milk cheese called tomino di Melle. It's a fresh cheese, which only needs to be matured for five days before it's ready to be used. Robiola cheese also from Piemonte is a good substitute, and if you cannot find that in your deli, any soft fresh cheese will do. Even a chèvre goat's cheese would be nice. Domenica advises to use the best possible alpine butter you can find for the dressing. This is a special occasion dish, traditionally served at baptisms and engagement parties. Thus the liberal use of butter is a treat!

FOR THE RAVIOLE

1 kg (2 lb 4 oz) old floury potatoes, unpeeled
200 g (7 oz) tomino di Melle or other fresh cheese (see introduction)
250 g (9 oz/2 cups) 0 flour or plain (all-purpose) flour
salt

TO SERVE

75 g (2½ oz) unsalted butter (actually, Domenica uses considerably more than this!)
100 ml (3½ fl oz/scant ½ cup) single (light) cream
grated Parmigiano Reggiano

Boil the potatoes in salted water. When they are cooked, drain and peel them. While still hot, put them through a potato ricer or vegetable mill and then spread the mash over a well-floured wooden board. Crumble or mash the tomino di Melle cheese and scatter it over the potatoes along with the flour. The hot mash will melt the cheese. Mix everything and knead it until the ingredients have blended together. Check for seasoning.

Chop up the dough into fist-size pieces, then roll each one out so it looks like a thick bread stick. Slice these into 3 cm (1¼ in) long pillows, then take each one and roll it along the board to create a short spindle shape, around 5–7 cm (about 2½ in) long.

Have a platter ready in a warming oven. Bring a large saucepan of water to the boil, add some salt and then return it to the boil. You will probably have to cook the ravioles in batches, as you don't want to overcrowd the pan. When they bob to the surface, scoop them out with a sieve or slotted spoon and place them on the warm platter.

In a small sauté pan, fry the butter until it is golden and smells nutty. Domenica goes further and aims for flecks of black at the bottom of the pan, but there is no need to do this. In another saucepan, warm through the cream.

Pour the melted butter, warmed cream and a handful of grated Parmigiano Reggiano over the cooked raviole. Some folk like to grill this briefly (make sure your platter is oven-proof if you want to do this step).

DOMENICA'S POTATO GNOCCHI WITH TOMATO SAUCE

FOR 6 PEOPLE

Memories of the Second World War still loom large in Montese, a town in the mountains to the south of Bologna. It was the scene of some intense fighting before being liberated by the Brazilians. Domenica told us a story of how her family sheltered a British soldier for several months, keeping him hidden behind their haystack. He eventually had to try and reach Allied lines and was sadly killed in his attempt. She still has his signet ring that he left with the family.

Domenica says the key to good gnocchi is to use the right potatoes. And she lives in the right place, as Montese is famous for its potatoes – it even has a DOP to protect them. Her ratio is 1 kg (2 lb 4 oz) of potatoes for every 300 g (9 oz/2 cups) of flour and, in Domenica's hands, this makes deliciously light gnocchi. No egg is needed in this recipe.

FOR THE GNOCCHI
1.5 kg (3 lb 5 oz) all-purpose potatoes, (peeled weight), around the same size
450 g (1 lb/3¾ cups) plain (all-purpose) flour

FOR THE TOMATO SAUCE
3 shallots, finely diced
1 carrot, finely diced
1 celery stick, finely diced
4 tablespoons extra-virgin olive oil or butter
400 g (14 oz) passata (sieved tomatoes) (Domenica makes her own)
salt

TO SERVE
30 g (1 oz) grated Parmigiano Reggiano (preferably aged for 24 months)

Quarter your potatoes – you want the pieces to be all the same size – and boil them until just tender. Drain them thoroughly and let the steam evaporate for a few minutes.

Heat the olive oil or butter in a large frying pan (skillet) over a low heat, and cook the diced veggies for around 10 minutes, until soft. Add the passata, season and leave the sauce to simmer gently.

Meanwhile, make the potato gnocchi. Make a well in the flour (Domenica uses a huge wooden board made from local chestnut wood as her work surface). Use a potato ricer to mash the potato into the centre of the flour. (Using a ricer gives a lighter texture than using a regular masher.) Fold and mix in the flour, then knead it for just long enough for the flour to disappear into the potato. Then stop. You don't want the gluten in the flour to develop.

Keeping everything well floured, take a chunk of the potato mash and roll it out to form a rope about 3 cm (1¼ in) in diameter. Then chop it up into little pillows – how big is up to you, but aim for something about two fingers-width wide. Use those two fingers to press very gently into the middle of each piece and roll it towards you at the same time. You want a chubby curl. Repeat until you have used all the potato.

Bring a large saucepan of salted water to the boil. Chuck in as many gnocchi as will fit comfortably (you may have to cook them in batches) and let them bob to the surface - it will take around 2 minutes. Scoop them out with a slotted spoon or sieve and add them to the tomato sauce. Fold in the gnocchi so they are coated with the sauce.

Serve immediately with a generous flourish of grated Parmigiano Reggiano.

QUINTINA'S GNOCCHETTI WITH CHICKPEAS

FOR 4 PEOPLE

Quintina is Ada's older sister (see page 88) and they live in neighbouring streets.

The Italian name for this dish is *gnocchetti con ceci*. Quintana's gnocchetti are an unusual but easy ingredient to add texture and interest to a chickpea soup. She lives high in the mountains of Abruzzo where pasta cooking water isn't poured down the sink but used as the base for the soup. Gnocchetti means tiny gnocchi, and they are the same size as the chickpeas with which they are served. In fact, in the neighbouring village of Ortona dei Marsi they are called *ciccerchie*, which is a play on the word for chickpeas in Italian: *ceci*.

Gnocchetti are made from a mixture of polenta and wheat flour. If your polenta is coarse, blitz it with a food processor to make it more flour-like.

FOR THE GNOCCHETTI
200 g (7 oz/1²/₃ cups) finely ground polenta
200 g (7 oz/1²/₃ cups) plain (all-purpose) flour
pinch of salt
about 200 ml (7 fl oz/scant 1 cup) warm water

FOR THE CONDIMENTO
500 g (1 lb 2 oz) cooked chickpeas (garbanzo beans) (250 g/9 oz dried weight if you are cooking them from scratch)
300 g (10½ oz/2½ cups) passata (sieved tomatoes), or the leftovers of a meat ragù (see Alba's recipe on pages 157–158)
3 tablespoons extra-virgin olive oil

TO SERVE
grated Pecorino

Mix all the gnocchetti ingredients together and give the dough a quick knead to make sure the flours are properly incorporated. It should be a soft but not sticky dough. There is no need to leave it to rest, simply roll it out so it's about 1 cm (½ in) thick. Cut the dough into 1 cm (½ in) wide strips, then line them up (if they have scattered) and chop them up to make little pea-sized balls. Keep them well floured while you make the sauce.

Heat the chickpeas in a saucepan with the passata. (It should have a similar consistency to the contents of a baked beans tin.)

Bring a large saucepan of salted water to the boil. Dump all the gnocchetti into the water and return it to a simmer. After a couple of minutes, they will bob to the surface, at which point they are cooked. Remove some of the water – how much will depend on how thin you like your soup. Stir through the chickpea mixture, with a slug of olive oil. Ladle out the soup into bowls, scattering some cheese over each serving.

SELVINA'S GNOCCHI CON SALSICCE

FOR 4 PEOPLE

For many years, Cremona was just one of those signs I saw on the motorway on the way to Milan, too busy worrying – teeth gritted, hands gripped on the steering wheel – about the tailgating speedster behind me to consider visiting. But it's definitely worth a detour: just outside, in a little village scattered along what feels like a Roman road to nowhere, lived Selvina Bertuzzi. She passed away in April 2019. I am most sorry she didn't get to see her story in this book.

We piled into her kitchen one Sunday morning in early spring to film Selvina making potato gnocchi. Selvina came across as shy and hesitant about making the dish, despite having cooked it for decades; her daughter, Oriana, gently helped out as sous chef. For this recipe, Selvina used to use a type of plain, unspiced sausage common in Lombardy called *luganica*. It's made without links, so you'll see it presented in a spiral.

FOR THE GNOCCHI
1 kg (2 lb 4 oz) old, floury potatoes
250 g (9 oz/2 cups) plain (all-purpose) flour
1 egg

FOR THE SAUCE
1 onion, finely chopped
1 tablespoon extra-virgin olive oil
4 good-quality plain sausages, skins removed
400g (14 oz) tin of tomatoes
salt

TO SERVE
grated Parmigiano Reggiano
knob of unsalted butter

Peel the potatoes and boil them whole or in halves. Leave them to cool just a little before passing the pieces through a potato ricer. Spread the mash out to let it cool further. You want warm, not steaming hot, potato.

Sprinkle the flour over the mash and crack in the egg. Mix it quickly and gently so everything amalgamates. Then stop – this is not like making bread or pasta. On a floured surface, roll the mixture into ropes and cut into pieces the size of large green olives.

In a frying pan (skillet), sauté the onion in olive oil until soft but not coloured. Crumble in the sausage meat and smash it down into the onion. Fry it for another couple of minutes and then add the tomatoes. Break up the tomatoes, season with salt and let it bubble down to a chunky sauce. This will take around 20–30 minutes.

When you're ready to cook your gnocchi, bring a large saucepan of salted water to the boil. Warm a serving platter and have it ready. Add the gnocchi to the water – in batches if necessary, depending on the size of your pan as you don't want to gnocchi to be overcrowded. Once they bob to the surface, wait another 30 seconds and then scoop them out with a sieve or slotted spoon. Place on the warmed dish, sprinkle the Parmigiano Reggiano over the top, then fold through the sauce, followed by a generous knob of butter. Eat immediately.

OLGA'S CANEDERLI

MAKES ABOUT 12 CANEDERLI,
ENOUGH FOR 4-6 PEOPLE

The town of Selva will be well known to those of you who are fans of skiing. It's a resort in the Dolomites, in an area which was for many years part of Austria. In fact, it doesn't feel like Italy at all, and this is reflected in its traditionally hearty food, including canederli – bread dumplings the size of oranges – from an era when a loaf of bread had to last several weeks. All the ingredients for this dish were the scraps left over from a better meal. Each household has its own take on the base recipe of smooshing bread together and simmering the balls in water or stock. Some add cheese, and there's even one version that includes brains . . .

Olga started making *canederli* with her mother, when she was 16. She says that when she was a young woman, if you didn't know how to cook you weren't considered good marriage material. This was something her mum told her regularly, so she ended up cooking in an alpine hostel for a season to improve her skills. This stood her in good stead, as she got married at 20, had three children and ran the family B&B for many years. Nowadays, her children have taken over the responsibility. Olga still likes to make canederli every Sunday, and often serves them with goulash. Alternatively, you could serve them with a green salad, melted butter and a shower of grated Parmigiano Reggiano.

3 tablespoons extra-virgin olive oil
   or butter, plus extra to serve
½ small onion, finely minced
50 g (2 oz) speck, diced small
500 g (1 lb 2 oz) stale white bread, cubed
3 eggs, beaten
200–250 ml (7–8½ fl oz/scant 1 cup–
   1 cup) milk
1 heaped tablespoon 00 flour or plain
   (all-purpose) flour
10 g (½ oz) chives, minced
salt

Heat the oil or butter in a frying pan (skillet) and sauté the onion over a low heat. When it is translucent, add the speck and sauté for 1 more minute, to warm it through but not to cook it; speck turns hard if you cook it, and you want it to remain soft. Take the pan off the heat.

Take a large bowl and add the bread, eggs, 200 ml (7 fl oz/scant 1 cup) milk then stir. Once combined, add the speck and oil, followed by the flour, a pinch

of salt and the chives. Continue to stir the mixture until the ingredients bind together. If the bread feels too dry, add some or all of the remaining milk. Let the mixture rest for about 15 minutes so the bread fully absorbs all the wet ingredients.

Bring a large pan of salted water to the boil. It should be deep enough to cover the canederli by three-quarters.

When the canederli is ready, have a bowl of water to one side. Wet your hands and scoop out a small handful of the mixture. Press it hard to make sure it binds together, then roll it between your palms in a circular motion and shape into a neat little ball. It should be the size of a clementine or small orange. Place it on a plate and repeat until all the mixture is used up.

Cook your canederli in batches. Lower them in the hot water and simmer for 10 minutes. You may need to turn the heat down a little, so the boil isn't too rapid. Keep them warm in a low oven while you cook the others. To serve, drizzle over some melted butter and eat straight away.

GIUSY'S 'NDUNDERI WITH TOMATO SAUCE

FOR 4–6 PEOPLE

Normally, our criteria for selecting our grannies is that they have to be real-life grannies, or over 60 – preferably over 70. We made an exception for Giusy, though, as she learned how to make *'ndunderi* from her nonna and has become an expert. Even though she was only 21 years old when we filmed her, she had already appeared on Italian TV demonstrating her skills.

'Ndunderi are ricotta gnocchi. Instead of the usual potato-flour combo, ricotta is the main ingredient. This makes them much lighter. They are a speciality of Minori on the Amalfi Coast. This can also be made in advance and frozen, cooked until the tomato sauce is bubbling and piping hot.

FOR THE 'NDUNDERI
250 g (9 oz) fresh cow's milk ricotta, drained
2 egg yolks, beaten
125 g (4 oz/1 cup) 00 flour or plain (all-purpose) flour (you may need a little more or less depending on how wet the ricotta is), plus more for dusting
40 g (1½ oz) grated Parmigiano Reggiano
pinch of salt
pinch of pepper
pinch of ground nutmeg
shredded basil, to serve

FOR THE TOMATO SAUCE
2 × 400 g (14 oz) tins plum tomatoes
1 onion, chopped
1 garlic clove, minced
1 bay leaf
3 tablespoons extra-virgin olive oil
1 teaspoon sugar
½ teaspoon salt
200 g (7 oz) smoked scamorza, provola or mozzarella
15 g (½ oz) grated Parmigiano Reggiano

Put the ricotta in a sieve over a bowl for 30 minutes, to make sure it's properly drained. Once the ricotta has drained, mix all the ingredients for the 'ndunderi together (apart from the basil). Knead the dough just long enough to incorporate everything thoroughly. Then stop. You're not trying to make pasta or bread here. Place the dough in a bowl and cover it with a tea towel (or use a lidded bowl) and chill it in the fridge for 30 minutes. This minimises the amount of flour you need as it's easier to handle.

Meanwhile, make the tomato sauce. Put all the ingredients except the cheeses in a saucepan. Fill a tomato tin with water and add this, too. Simmer for 40 minutes or so, until the tomatoes have broken down, the onion is soft and the sauce is nice and chunky. Remove the bay leaf, then blitz together with a hand-held blender.

When the dough has chilled, divide the mixture in half. You're looking to make plump little dumplings the size of walnuts, so roll out one portion into a thick rope about 2.5 cm (1 in) in diameter before chopping it up. Aim for even-sized pieces so they'll cook through in the same amount of time. You should end up with about 30 dumplings.

Dust the prongs of a large fork with flour (choose a fork with long prongs, as it makes rolling easier) and gently roll each ricotta ball along the tines, to make a nice ridged dumpling. Place them on a floured surface while you make the others. Then repeat with the other portion of dough.

When you are ready to cook the 'ndunderi, add half the smoked scamorza to the sauce and continue cooking it until the cheese has melted.

Preheat the oven to 200°C (400°F/gas mark 6).

Bring a large pan of salted water to the boil and plop in the 'ndunderi. Simmer for 5 minutes – they will bob to the top of the water when cooked. If your dumplings are on the large size, you will need to simmer them for longer, say 7 minutes in total. Use slotted spoon or sieve to transfer them to the tomato sauce. Cook for 1 minute before transferring the mixture to a 25 × 30 cm (10 × 12 in) gratin dish.

Scatter over the remaining scamorza and the Parmigiano Reggiano and bake for 10 minutes – or until the cheeses have melted. Spoon into bowls and serve with shredded basil.

LUCIA'S SAGNE WITH BREADCRUMB DUMPLINGS

FOR 6 PEOPLE

Lucia from Presicce in Puglia was born in 1930, the only daughter among seven sons. Her mother accidentally stabbed herself with a needle and developed an infection, which caused her to have her arm amputated. Lucia, therefore, had to cook for her family from an early age: 'You can imagine how much pasta I made! I learned through practise – my brothers would tell me too much salt! Not enough salt!'

'You have to have a passion for food,' Lucia says. 'And if you have good ingredients, you don't need to worry about cooking or following a recipe because they do the work for you. But, just as important is you should sit down as family to eat together – you know, we even ate breakfast together. That doesn't happen so often nowadays.' Here Lucia shares her recipe for mint-flavoured breadcrumb dumplings called *susciella*.

FOR THE PASTA
400 g (14 oz/3⅓ cups) finely ground
    semolina flour
200 ml (7 fl oz/scant 1 cup) tepid water

FOR THE TOMATO SAUCE
4 tablespoons extra-virgin olive oil
1 onion, diced
800 g (1 lb 12 oz) passata
    (sieved tomatoes)
1 bay leaf
salt

FOR THE SUSCIELLA
250 g (9 oz) cow's milk ricotta
3 eggs
20 g (¾ oz) mint, leaves stripped from
    the stalk and chopped
130 g (4 oz) breadcrumbs
25 g (¾ oz) grated Pecorino

FOR THE FRIED SUSCIELLA (OPTIONAL)
saucer of breadcrumbs (to roll the
    susciella in)
vegetable oil, for frying

First, prepare your tomato sauce. Heat the olive oil in a large sauté pan and cook the onion for around 10 minutes, until it has softened. Empty the passata into the pan, then rinse out the bottle with water and add this to the mixture. Add the bay leaf and a pinch of salt, to taste. Leave it to simmer for as long as possible – over an hour – to bring out the sweetness of the tomato. Remove the bay leaf and blitz the sauce with a hand-held blender.

Make the pasta dough as described on page 21. After it has rested for 10 minutes, roll it out to 2–3 mm thick. Slice it into ribbons about 2 cm (¾ in) wide. Grab a ribbon at one end and roll the other end so it twists. Fold it in half if it is a long piece and place it on a tray. Repeat until you have twisted all your sagne.

For the susciella, mash all the ingredients together. The mixture should stand to attention and not fall from the fork when you lift some out of the bowl; if it does, add more breadcrumbs. Wet your hands and take an apricot-sized piece of the mixture and roll it between your palms then gently flatten it. This will make around 15 patties. You can either poach them all in the tomato sauce, or for textural interest, fry some of them.

To poach the susciella, place them in the tomato sauce and cook them for 5 minutes. If you are frying some, roll the patties in breadcrumbs. Heat some vegetable oil in a frying pan (skillet) – test the heat by adding a few crumbs; if they sizzle immediately, the oil is hot enough. Fry the dumplings until they are golden on both sides. Just before serving, place them into the tomato sauce alongside the poached ones.

To assemble the dish, bring a large pan of salted water to the boil. Add the sagne and let them simmer for around 3 minutes – test one to ensure its cooked.

Drain the pasta into a bowl and and ladle over tomato sauce and susciella. Serve immediately.

ROSA'S SPINACH AND RICOTTA GNUDI

———

FOR 2 PEOPLE

Rosa is the matriarch of the pasta-making Martelli family and she shared her recipe for *gnudi* after we had visited their factory. Gnudi means nude, and it alludes to these dumplings being pasta-less – they are ravioli without their coats. Gnudi are typical of Tuscany, where the Martelli factory is. Rosa says it's important that the spinach and ricotta are as dry as you can make them, otherwise they will disintegrate in cooking.

For this recipe, you will need to buy two pots of ricotta – usually about 200 g (7 oz) net weight each – because the drained weight will be less than this. This recipe also works well with young chard, with the thicker stems removed.

FOR THE GNUDI
250 g (9 oz) cow's milk ricotta, drained weight
600 g (1 lb 5 oz) spinach
25 g (¾ oz) finely grated Parmigiano Reggiano
1 large egg, beaten
plain (all-purpose) flour, for rolling and dusting
salt

FOR THE DRESSING
30 g (1 oz) unsalted butter
5 sage leaves
several scrapes of nutmeg

TO SERVE
2 tablespoons grated Parmigiano Reggiano

Place the ricotta in a sieve over a bowl and leave it to drain for an hour or so, then weigh out 250 g (9 oz).

Meanwhile, place the spinach leaves in a saucepan, turn the heat up to high and add 2 tablespoons of boiling water. Cover the pan with its lid and steam the spinach until it has collapsed. Drain the spinach through a sieve and leave it to cool. Squeeze out as much water as possible and roughly chop. You should end up with about 300 g (10½ oz) cooked spinach.

Mix the spinach with the ricotta, Parmigiano Reggiano and beaten egg. Season to taste. Make sure the ingredients are all playing nicely together.

Pour some flour into a bowl. Pinch off 20 g (¾ oz) pieces of the mixture (about the size of a large walnut) and toss each one in the flour before rolling it between your palms to create a nice little ball. Dust off any excess flour. Place on a lightly floured board, away from each other so they don't stick.

Have a frying pan (skillet) on one side of your stove, and a sauté pan on the other. Melt the butter in the frying pan with the sage and nutmeg and keep it warm while you cook the gnudi.

Fill a sauté pan with salted water and bring to a gentle simmer. Lower the gnudi gently into the pan and let them tremble in the water for 5 minutes, or until they bob to the surface. Use a slotted spoon to transfer them to the butter in the frying pan. You may have to cook the gnudi in batches.

Spoon the butter over the gnudi, then serve them with a shower of grated cheese over the top.

five

Seafood

Italy is blessed with a long coastline and every port and fishing village has its own seafood speciality. And anchovies, of course, crop up everywhere in Italian cooking! The best thing to do with a fresh fish is to cook it as simply as possible; using the shells and bones for a tasty broth or soup. Hence there are not lots of recipes pairing fish and pasta, but shellfish often find their way into a plate of pasta.

RACHELE'S MACCHERONI A DESCITA WITH CUTTLEFISH

———

FOR 4-6 PEOPLE

Ninety-six-year-old Rachele's husband Gerardo decided to declare his love for her when he was 17. He picked the most luscious, ripe grapes he could find and asked a family friend to give them to her with the words: 'If you think these grapes are sweet, think about how sweet the man who gave them to you is.' Rachele, indeed, found them to be the sweetest grapes she had ever tasted, and they were inseparable from that moment on.

When I asked Rachele about her favourite food, she shrugged and said 'When you are poor, it really doesn't matter what you eat, as long as you eat something. I do enjoy making *maccheroni a descita*, they are fun.' This version is a Christmas dish in Sant' Agata, where Rachele now lives. She uses cuttlefish as it tends to travel rather better than other fish, plus it is much cheaper. If you can not find cuttlefish, substitute it with squid.

THE PASTA

400 g (14 oz/3⅓ cups) 00 flour or plain (all-purpose) flour (or you could also use finely ground semolina flour for a chewier pasta)

180-200 ml (6-7 fl oz/¾-scant 1 cup) water

FOR THE CUTTLEFISH

200 g (7 oz) breadcrumbs made from bread that is a few days old

2 garlic cloves, chopped

1 tablespoon chopped parsley

1 tablespoon extra-virgin olive oil, plus extra to fry

about 4 tablespoons milk

1 large cuttlefish (about 600 g/1 lb 7 oz), cleaned

400 g (14 oz) passata (sieved tomatoes), plus a little water

salt

FOR THE TOPPING

150 g (5 oz) breadcrumbs

1 tablespoon chopped parsley

1 garlic clove, minced

extra-virgin olive oil, to fry the mixture

Prepare the cuttlefish. Mix the breadcrumbs, garlic, parsley and oil together in a bowl. Add the milk a little at a time – it should be moist, but not dripping. Snip the cuttlefish tentacles into very small pieces and add these to the breadcrumbs, then stuff the mixture into the cuttlefish cavity.

Thread a metal skewer through the cavity opening to close it up. Rachele's daughter Domenica says people once used a needle and thread.

Choose a saucepan into which the cuttlefish will fit snugly. Heat a puddle of olive oil over a medium heat and add the cuttlefish. Sauté for 10 minutes, before adding the passata. Half fill your tin or bottle with water, swirl it around to rinse the final traces of tomato and pour this in. Season with salt. Cover the pan with a lid and leave it to simmer for about 1 hour, until the cuttlefish is tender. Check the liquid occasionally and add a little more water if necessary.

Meanwhile, to make the topping, mix the breadcrumbs with the parsley and garlic. Pour enough olive oil to cover the base of your frying pan (skillet). Heat it over a gentle heat and then sauté the crumbs until they are golden and crisp. You will need to stir it frequently and it will take around 10 minutes. Put to one side.

Make the pasta dough as described on page 21.

Pull off pieces of dough, each about 100 g (3½ oz). Roll them out into a thick rope, and then cut into 3-4 cm (1¼-1½ in) lengths. Take each piece and, using your middle fingers, press into the dough and pull it towards you, pressing down onto the board. You'll end up with a curled gnocchi shape. Repeat until you have used up all the dough.

Bring a large pan of salted water to the boil then add the maccheroni a descita and give them a stir. When they start to bob to the surface they are almost ready – cook for a further minute more. Taste for doneness. Continue cooking for as long as you think necessary – it will depend on the size and thickness of your pasta.

Remove the cuttlefish from the tomato sauce, and slice it. Reserve some of the tomato sauce for the cuttlefish. Drain the pasta and mix it with the tomato sauce. Sprinkle the fried breadcrumbs over each serving of the pasta and eat promptly. Serve the cuttlefish afterwards, dressed in the reserved tomato sauce. In Italy this is the secondo – the main course.

LINA'S TACCUNA WITH TUNA, ARTICHOKES AND PRAWNS

FOR 6 PEOPLE

Seventy-year-old Lina doesn't call herself a chef: 'I do home cooking,' she says of the food she serves in her little restaurant Taverna Cialoma in Marzamemi, Sicily. It has Greek-blue window frames and inside it is all apricot-orange and azure Sicilian tiles and vintage lace. There's a deck out the back, where you can eat, with waves gently sloshing a metre away from your table. We visited her one spring morning, just before the tuna season had started, so she used a fish called *palamita* – Atlantic bonito – for her pasta dish. It has a similar firm flesh and flavour to tuna, so you could use this if you prefer.

Lina uses freshly milled heritage durum wheat flour from Sicily for her *taccuna* pasta, which gave it the most wonderful nutty aroma and rough texture – try and find something similar.

FOR THE PASTA
600 g (1 lb 7 oz/3½ cups) finely ground
   semolina flour (preferably a heritage
   wheat variety), plus extra to toss
270–300 ml (9–10 fl oz/1–1¼ cups)
   tepid water

FOR THE FISH AND ARTICHOKE SAUCE
1 lemon
6 large artichokes
4 tablespoons extra-virgin olive oil
1 large garlic clove
3 generous tablespoons finely chopped
   parsley
300 g (10½ oz) palamita or tuna fillet,
   cut into 3 cm (1¼ in) dice
pinch of peperoncino
12 raw prawns (shrimp)
20 g (¾ oz) grated Parmigiano Reggiano
   (preferably aged for 30 months)
salt

Make the pasta as described on page 21. Roll it out until it is 2 mm thick, then cut into stubby ribbons, about 2.5 cm (1 in) wide and 15 cm (6 in) long. Toss the pasta with a little semolina flour and leave them while you prep the fish and artichoke sauce (they don't need to be covered).

Artichokes discolour rapidly when exposed to the air, so fill a bowl with water and squeeze the lemon juice into it. Then add the lemon halves for good measure. Prepare the artichokes as described on page 72 (leaving the stalks intact, and the artichokes unsliced). Place the artichokes in the lemony water as soon as you have finished prepping each one.

When you have prepped them all, transfer the water and artichokes (not the lemon) to a saucepan and arrange the artichokes so the stalks are sticking out of the water. Add a teaspoon of salt, cover the pan with its lid and leave it to simmer gently for about 30 minutes, until the artichokes are tender. To check they are done, poke a knife into one; it should have no resistance. Once they are cooked, drain them and slice them lengthways in 6 pieces.

Bring a large saucepan of salted water to the boil for the pasta. While it's heating up, make the fish sauce.

Warm the olive oil in a sauté pan over a medium to high heat. Add the whole garlic clove and the chopped parsley, followed by the pieces of fish. Season with a pinch of salt and peperoncino. Fry briskly for around 3 minutes, flipping the fish over with a spatula halfway through cooking, until the flesh has turned white.

Stir in the prepared artichoke slices and continue cooking until the fish is cooked through. Remove the garlic clove.

Throw the pasta into the boiling water and cook for about 4 minutes – nibble one to check its progress. Use a slotted spoon or sieve to scoop out the pasta and into the fish mixture. Plop the prawns into the pasta water to cook – they will turn pink in about a minute. Drain and add to the pasta.

Toss the fish, pasta and prawns together with the Parmigiano Reggiano. Serve immediately, preferably in the sunshine.

Lina uses freshly milled heritage durum
wheat flour from Sicily for her taccuna
pasta, which gave it the most wonderful
nutty aroma and rough texture – try and
find something similar.

ROSETTA'S PASTA WITH SARDINES

FOR 6 PEOPLE

The version of pasta *con le sarde* that most people come across is from Palermo. This one is from Caltabellotta, a village situated 900 metres above sea level, and it is from a time when the local farmers were also fishermen. This dish is mostly eaten on St Joseph's Day, on 19 March (also Father's Day in Italy) and at Easter, because March is when the sardines are plump and the fennel fronds are fluffy.

The recipe involves several stages, some of which can be out-sourced: buying your sardines already gutted and filleted by your fishmonger is one I recommend. And the pasta can be bought, too! Rosetta used a curled thin macaroni pasta called *ruvidelli*, but *bucatini* will also work. Rosetta also uses her own tomato paste which is called *strattu* in Sicilian. Every July, she spreads salted tomato pulp over a wood board to dry in the sun for four or five days.

150 g (5 oz) very fine breadcrumbs
1 tablespoon caster (superfine) sugar
500 g (1 lb 2 oz) wild fennel (a nice bunch)
1 onion
4 tablespoons extra-virgin olive oil
1 garlic clove
6 anchovy fillets
200 g (7 oz) passata (sieved tomatoes)
3 heaped tablespoons tomato purée
18 plump sardine fillets, gutted and filleted
plain (all-purpose) flour, for dusting
vegetable oil, for frying
500 g (1 lb 2 oz) dried pasta (ruvidelli, or similar)
salt

Heat a non-stick frying pan (skillet) and add in the breadcrumbs with the sugar. Keep stirring, until the breadcrumbs change colour from pale to golden chestnut. Put to one side.

Bring a large saucepan of water to the boil and cook the wild fennel for about 10 minutes, until the main stalks are tender. Keeping the hot water for cooking the pasta, scoop out the fennel with a slotted spoon or sieve and chop it up.

Make a rich tomato sauce by frying the onion in the olive oil in a large sauté pan for around 7 minutes until it is soft, then add the garlic. A minute later, mush the anchovies into the onion mix with a wooden spoon. Stir in the passata, tomato purée and two-thirds of the cooked fennel. Taste the sauce and add some salt, if necessary. Pour in 200 ml (7 fl oz/ scant 1 cup) water then let the mixture slowly reduce for an hour or so. Towards the end of cooking time, add 6 sardine fillets to the sauce.

Dust the remaining 12 sardine fillets in flour. Heat a small pan with a good puddle of vegetable oil (Rosetta in fact uses olive oil). She says you'll know it's hot enough when you place the end of a tooth pick into the oil and it sizzles.

Fry the floured sardines a few a time, placing them on kitchen paper while you work through the rest. The fillets will only need a minute or so on each side to cook.

Bring the fennel water back up to the boil and cook the pasta, following the manufacturer's instructions. Drain it and toss with the tomato sauce.

Ladle out the pasta into warmed bowls, add 2 fried sardines per serving, some chopped fennel and a sprinkling of the sugared breadcrumbs.

BEATRICE'S BARLEY MACCHERONI WITH SEAFOOD

—

FOR 6 PEOPLE

Beatrice lives in Patu at the very tip of southern Italy. She left school when she was 10 because her mother was ill, so she could help her grandmother cook and look after her siblings. 'I love cooking,' she says. 'It's a way of showing your love and getting everyone together. Even now, I have a brother in Switzerland and a sister in northern Italy, and they all come home in springtime, just before the poppies bloom. We pick them, wash them five or six times and fry them with olive oil and garlic to make a kind of paste. We all sit down and eat it on bread, it's a kind of family heaven.'

'When I was a kid, the only time you ate fish or meat was at big celebrations or if you were ill. Beans and vegetables are still the food I love to eat the most. And, of course, pasta. Barley flour is very difficult to manage – but it's better if you put a little bit of semolina into the mix.'

When Beatrice made *minchiareddi* (the local nickname for maccheroni – it means little penises!), she used 100 per cent barley flour and it was crumbly and hard work thanks to the low gluten levels. You have been warned! If you want to be very modern, try adding a couple of tablespoons of gluten flour as it will make kneading much easier. And if you are inexperienced, use a 50/50 mix of barley and finely ground semolina. Why bother with barley flour, you may ask? Well, its nutty taste goes very well with seafood.

Beatrice used winter tomatoes – she had harvested them the previous summer, strung them up in the shade and 7 months later they were still delicious, thanks to their thick skin.

To make this shape you will need a square-sided rod or stick about the same dimensions as a skewer (but without the handle). Italians in the south can buy a metal one, hence the word *ferro*, which means 'iron' in Italian, and the rest of us have to find something similar. It can be wood or metal: an umbrella spoke, a skewer, dowel, dried grass stem (see Angela's recipe on page 52) or twig (see Violetta on page 185). If you use a smooth, rounded rod, like a knitting needle, the pasta will tend to stick.

Recipe method overleaf

FOR THE PASTA

500 g (1 lb 2 oz/4 cups) barley flour
100 g (3½ oz) finely ground semolina
    flour
270–300 ml (9–10 fl oz/1–1¼ cups) water

FOR THE SEAFOOD RAGÙ

4 tablespoons extra-virgin olive oil
1 garlic clove, minced
500 g (1 lb 2 oz) squid, cleaned and cut
    into thin strips
400 g (14 oz) mussels, cleaned and
    de-bearded
400 g (14 oz) clams
8 large prawns (shrimp)
250 g (9 oz) fresh tomatoes, halved
100 ml (3½ fl oz/scant ½ cup) white wine
salt

TO SERVE

4 tablespoons chopped parsley

Mix the flours together either in a bowl or on a board. Add the water and mix in the flours to make a dough. Knead it for a good 10 minutes – this dough needs a really thorough kneading. If it stays crumbly, add more semolina flour. Keep going until you have a dough that is soft but not sticky. Cover it with a tea towel (or put it in a lidded bowl) and leave it to rest for 30 minutes.

Taking one chunk of dough at a time, roll it into rope. Chop it into 3 cm (1¼ in) long pieces. Take one piece of pasta and place it on the board. Press your ferro flat along its length. Holding the ferro with your left hand (if you are right-handed), with the flat of your other hand, roll it back and forth over the pasta and across the board. You are trying to roll the pasta around the ferro to form a tube. If it doesn't close completely, don't worry it will still taste the same, but keep practising.

To make the seafood ragù, use a large sauté pan – a wok is a good substitute. Heat the oil and briefly fry the garlic before adding the seafood, tomatoes and wine. Cover with a lid and leave it to steam for 5 minutes. Discard any mussels or clams that haven't opened, then give everything a good shake.

Bring a large saucepan of salted water to the boil. Add your pasta and simmer for 4–5 minutes – taste a piece to check for doneness.

Since they are not the most robust pasta, use a slotted spoon or sieve to scoop them from the pan straight into the ragù; don't dump them into a colander in the sink. Check for seasoning, and give everything a good stir.

Sprinkle with the parsley and serve immediately. No cheese is needed.

VANDA'S TAGLIOLINI WITH SHRIMP

FOR 4 PEOPLE

One of my favourite restaurants in Italy is La Capanna di Eraclio – Eraclio's Hut. It's in the middle of the Po Delta, where roads and ditches run tandem with each other and the sky's so big you can practically see the curvature of the earth. Not so long ago, it teemed with labourers toiling in the huge fields, and on the corner of one stood Eraclio's family home. Life was tough. One pigeon had to flavour a meal for eight people, and sometimes they had singalongs to distract them from the fact there wasn't enough food for the family to eat.

The family had to be entrepreneurial, so they started by being the local *alimentari* – the grocer's shop. Then a brother became the local 'bike-smith', while a sister was the hairdresser. The alimentari started selling lunchtime snacks and it gradually evolved into a restaurant. Today, it has a Michelin star, but the atmosphere and decor remain homely. Eraclio was Vanda's father-in-law; she arrived, a young bride from Mantua, and went straight into working in the kitchen.

At 89 years old Vanda can still heave coal onto the open range where fish is grilled. And her morning always starts with making pasta – a routine she has kept for over 60 years. Daughter and chef, Maria Grazia, made the condimento with a local crustacean called *canocchie* (mantis shrimp). It is very similar to prawn in its flavour, but has a slightly softer texture. If you don't live on the Adriatic coastline, then use any raw prawn (shrimp) that is in season where you live. Vanda and Maria say *tagliolini* are often served with a seafood dressing – they are thin tagliatelle and should be 3 mm wide. Using a straight-bladed, large, very sharp knife makes this task easier.

Recipe method overleaf

FOR THE PASTA

400 g (14 oz/3⅓ cups) finely ground
    semolina flour
4 eggs

FOR THE MANTIS SHRIMP

800 g (1 lb 12 oz) raw mantis shrimp
    or prawns (in their shells)
½ teaspoon ground fennel seeds
1 tablespoon anise-flavoured alcohol
ice cubes
2 tablespoons extra-virgin olive oil
1 fresh red chilli sliced (adjust to your
    heat tolerance)
1 garlic clove
salt

TO SERVE

chopped parsley

Using semolina flour with eggs makes a very firm pasta dough – make it in the same way as described for the egg-based pasta on page 18. Traditionally, in this part of Italy, cooks would have used soft wheat flour.

Roll out the dough to a thickness of 1 mm. Leave the sfoglia to dry out a little. How long you leave it will depend on the temperature and humidity of your kitchen – you don't want it to stick together, but at the same time you don't want it to crack when rolled. Vanda left her dough for 10 minutes with the ceiling fan on.

Flour the dough and roll it over from each side, so the rolls meet in the middle (like a double scroll). Then fold one over the other and use a sharp, long-bladed knife to cut across the pasta to create folded over ribbons about 3 mm wide. Shake them out as you go along. Divide the pasta into 4 portions and twist the tagliolini into 4 nests. They can be left on a board while you make the sauce.

Blanch the shrimp in a pan of boiling water until they just turn pink – it will take about 1 minute. Drain, and when they're cool enough to handle, remove the shells. (If you are dealing with mantis shrimp, you will need a pair of scissors to snip down both sides of the carapace, before extracting the flesh.)

Place the shells in a saucepan with the ground fennel and the anise-flavoured alcohol. Cover with a layer of ice cubes and place the lid on top. Leave everything to simmer gently on a very low heat for around 45 minutes. This method extracts the maximum flavour from the shells. Strain and discard the shells. Reduce the stock to about 100 ml (3½ fl oz).

Boil a large saucepan of salted water, ready to cook the pasta, and warm 4 serving plates. While the water is heating up, heat the oil in a large frying pan (skillet) and cook the chilli and garlic for 3–4 minutes until the garlic softens but doesn't colour. Remove the garlic and add the shrimp flesh and stock and give it a 30 second stir-fry.

Part-cook the pasta in the boiling water for 1 minute. Drain it and add to the frying pan. Stir it through the shrimp sauce for another minute and check the seasoning. Divide between the warmed plates and scatter with some parsley.

Eat immediately.

ROSA'S MACCHERONI WITH SALT COD AND DRIED RED PEPPERS

FOR 6 PEOPLE

Rosa lives in the centro storico of a village called Sant'Arcangelo in Basilicata, high above the valley floor where her large vegetable garden and fruit orchard are. She is a market gardener – a *contadina*.

This unusual combination of pepper and salt cod is apparently from the 17th century, when the wealthy families of Basilicata ate this dish on their meat-free days. One can buy ready-prepared salt cod these days, but if you can only get hold of the stiff-as-old-shoe-leather kind of salt cod, you will have to soak it for a couple of days in plenty of cold water, changing the water every four to six hours. The dried red peppers can also be eaten like crisps, or scattered over other dishes.

FOR THE PASTA
600 g (1 lb 7 oz/3½ cups) finely ground
  semolina flour
270–300 ml (9–10 fl oz/1–1¼ cups) water

FOR THE BACCALA
4 tablespoons extra-virgin olive oil
2 garlic cloves
6 peperoni cruschi or other dried
  peppers
500 g (1 lb 2 oz) salt cod, rehydrated and
  cut into matchbox-sized pieces
2 tablespoons ground peperoni cruschi
  or mild unsmoked paprika
6 salted anchovies, deboned and rinsed,
  chopped

Make the dough as described on page 21, then leave it to rest for 30 minutes.

To make the maccheroni, pull off a piece of dough and roll it into a rope about 1 cm (½ in) in diameter. Slice it into 3 cm (1¼ in) lengths. Rosa likes to wrap these loosely round the ferro. Holding the ferro with your left hand (if you are right-handed), with the flat of your other hand, roll it back and forth over the pasta and across the board. You should form a tube with the pasta – don't worry if you can see the seam. Repeat until you have used all the dough. Once you have made them, place them on a tea towel, spread out, to dry a little.

Bring a large saucepan of salted water to the boil, ready for the pasta.

Add the olive oil to a large frying pan (skillet). The oil needs to be hot, but start cooking before it begins to shimmer. Add the garlic cloves followed by the dried peppers – they will crisp up very rapidly. Remove the peppers and place on some kitchen paper to drain.

Next, add the salt cod to the oil and sauté the pieces for 5 minutes, then remove the garlic cloves. While the salt cod is frying, boil the maccheroni for 5 minutes. Use a slotted spoon to remove the cod pieces and put them to one side while you add the paprika to the oil. Add a ladle of pasta water, scoop the maccheroni into the pan and continue to cook it for another couple of minutes. Return the cod to the frying pan along with the anchovies. Toss everything together.

Plate up the pasta and crumble the fried peppers over each serving.

TERESA'S MUSSELS WITH 'MARITATI' PASTA

FOR 4 PEOPLE

Teresa lives in the very south of Puglia where mussels are plentiful. She is an expert at prizing open the tightly closed bivalves, as she wants them shelled and raw before cooking them. Hers is not the standard approach (in the UK at least) to dealing with mussels, but she's 93 years old, and the method has served her well so far. *Maritati*, meanwhile, means 'married' in Italian; the name is given to a mixture of orecchiette and minchiareddi pastas, which are supposed to represent female and male shapes. Feel free to use only one or the other, but the mix is fun. Mussels are so easy to prepare, but can be quite daunting for most home cooks. Simply look for any with cracked shells or refuse to close when tapped. Discard those that don't close and are damaged.

FOR THE PASTA
400 g (14 oz/3⅓ cups) semolina flour
180–200 ml (6–7 fl oz/⅔–1 cup) warm
   water

FOR THE MUSSEL DRESSING
2 kg (4 lb 6 oz) fresh mussels
4 tablespoons extra-virgin olive oil
3 garlic cloves, halved
1 green chilli, thinly sliced
500 ml (17 fl oz/2 cups) passata
   (sieved tomatoes)
1 teaspoon salt

TO SERVE
2 tablespoons chopped parsley

Make the pasta dough as described on page 21. Use half the dough to make the orecchiette. Roll the dough into a long sausage, 1 cm (½ in) in diameter, then cut it into 1 cm (½ in) nuggets. Start at the edge furthest away from you and drag a blunt eating knife towards you over a nugget of dough, so it curls over the knife. Gently pull the dough off the knife, push your thumb inside and turn it inside out. Repeat the process until all the nuggets of dough have been used up. Make the maccheroni using the other half of dough, as described on pages 139–140. Set aside.

Next, prepare the mussels. Check for any with cracked shells or refuse to close when tapped, then discard. Scrape off any filaments and the mussel beard. Protect the hand with which you are going to

hold the mussel with a towel; you want to cut the mussel in two while holding the shells shut, so slide the knife blade into the join and slide it from one side to the other. Keep the mussel horizontal to stop the juices from spilling. Pour the juices into a bowl and scrape out the mussel. Repeat with the rest of the mussels, but leave 8 in their shells, just removing the top, for decoration. If you don't want to shuck your mussels before cooking, take a large, lidded saucepan, add 1 tablespoon of the olive oil and heat it over a medium to high heat. Once hot, dump the mussels into the pan and cover. Cook for 3 minutes. They should all have opened. Take the pan off the heat, and when the mussels are cool enough to handle, scrape the meat from the shells, keeping 8 for decoration. Reserve the cooking liquid.

Heat the remaining olive oil in a frying pan (skillet) over a medium heat. Add the garlic and chilli and fry before adding the passata and the salt. Stir and let it simmer for around 20 minutes.

While the sauce is cooking, add the pasta to a large pot of boiling salted water and cook for about 5 minutes. Check for doneness, then drain.

Add the raw mussels with their juices to the tomato sauce and place the shelled mussels on top. Cook for 3–4 minutes, then remove the garlic cloves. If you have already cooked your mussels, stir them through the tomato sauce just before mixing it with the pasta.

To serve, layer the pasta with the sauce on a serving platter and sprinkle over the parsley. Arrange the shelled mussels prettily on top and tuck in!

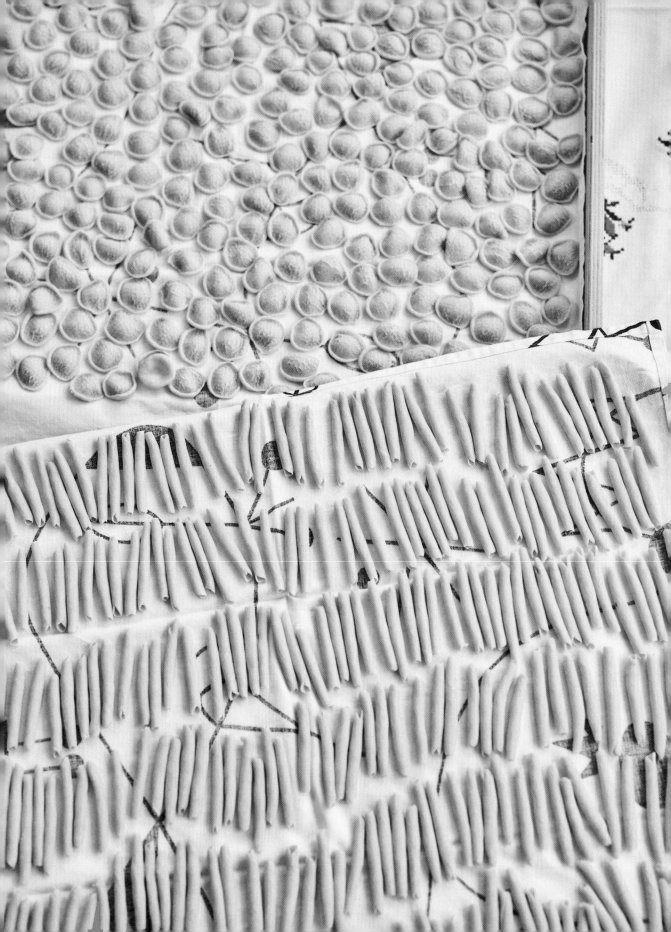

six

Meat

Traditionally, meat was something most people could not afford and so these recipes are celebration dishes for the one or two times a year – usually weddings, Easter or Christmas – when it was served. And pasta is a great way of making something precious go further. Nowadays, folk eat these dishes as often as the cook in their family is prepared to make the pasta. In this chapter I have put together a variety of cooking methods and meats from all over Italy.

FRANCA'S CLASSIC LASAGNA WITH BOLOGNESE

FOR 8 PEOPLE

Franca is a *contadina* – a market gardener – who lives in the hills to the south of Bologna. Her vegetables are organically grown, and for pasta-making she likes to use stone-ground, heritage wheat. This gives a rougher texture to the sfoglia. Franca stood in for another nonna who managed to injure her shoulder just before meeting us, saving the day. Sometimes our lovely ladies change their minds about being filmed or fall ill – we even had one who hurt her back cleaning her kitchen in preparation for our arrival. Franca, despite the short notice, produced her lasagna with great aplomb. She says, 'Remember this is a pasta dish; the meat ragù has a supporting role, so be sparing with it when you assemble the lasagna. To be a proper lasagna bolognese there should be at least five layers of pasta!'

FOR THE PASTA
400 g (14 oz/3⅓ cups) 00 flour or plain
(all-purpose) flour
4 eggs

FOR THE RAGÙ
4 tablespoons extra-virgin olive oil
3 celery sticks, finely diced
2 carrots, finely diced
1 onion, finely diced
150 g (5 oz) unsmoked pancetta
500 g (1 lb 2 oz) ground beef
500 g (1 lb 2 oz) ground pork
75 ml (2½ fl oz/5 tablespoons)
white wine
680 g (1 lb 8 oz) passata
(sieved tomatoes)
salt

FOR THE BÉCHAMEL
60 g (2 oz) butter
60 g (2 oz) plain (all-purpose) flour
1 litre (34 fl oz/4 cups) milk
freshly grated nutmeg (to taste)
salt and pepper

TO ASSEMBLE THE DISH
lots of grated Parmigiano Reggiano

For the ragù, heat the olive oil in a pan over a medium heat and add the celery, carrots and onion. Fry gently until the onion is translucent and the vegetables begin to soften.

Dice the pancetta into a rough paste – Franca likes to use a mezzaluna. Add this to the vegetables, followed by the ground beef, ground pork and wine. Season with a good pinch of salt. Cook for a few minutes, stirring and breaking up the mince with a wooden spoon, until the wine has evaporated. Add the passata and leave the ragù to simmer slowly for 2 hours, stirring every so often. At the end of cooking,

the ragù should be dark and thick; the tomato flavour will have lost its acidity and turned sweet.

While the ragù is cooking, make the pasta as described on page 18. Roll out the dough to a thickness of 1 mm. Cut the sfoglia into manageable rectangles, which are about one-third to a half of the size of your baking dish – which should be about 40 × 30 × 7 cm (16 × 12 × 3 in).

To make the béchamel, melt the butter in a saucepan. Add the flour, whisking continuously, to form a roux and cook for 2 minutes. Slowly, a little at a time, pour in the milk, continuing to whisk to avoid any lumps. When all the milk is used, bring the mixture to the boil, whisking constantly, until it has turned in to a thickish sauce, like custard. Season with nutmeg, salt and pepper to taste, and set aside.

When the ragù is ready, cook the pasta. Bring a large pan of salted water to the boil. Have a large pot of cold water on standby. Carefully drop 2 or 3 sheets of pasta into the boiling water for a couple of minutes, remove with a slotted spoon and immediately dunk in the cold water to stop them cooking further. Transfer the cooked sheets to a clean tea towel and pat dry.

Preheat the oven to 180°C (350°F/gas 4). To assemble the lasagna, ladle a thin layer of ragù on the bottom of the baking dish. Top with a layer of pasta – you may need to trim some of the sheets to form one single layer so as not to overlap them too much. Follow this with another layer of ragù – be more generous this time; using the back of the spoon push it right to the edge. Follow with a layer of béchamel then sprinkle over a generous handful of grated cheese. Repeat these steps (pasta, ragù, béchamel and cheese) to use up both sauces and the pasta. There should be at least 5 layers of pasta and the top should be sprinkled with cheese.

Cook the lasagna for 40 minutes. Remove from the oven and leave to stand for at least 15 minutes before slicing up for serving.

ALBA'S TAGLIATELLE WITH RAGÙ

———

FOR 4 PEOPLE

I expect you have your own recipe for spaghetti bolognese. Good old 'spag bol' is a popular dish everywhere but Italy – where it's unheard of, because everyone knows meat ragù is served with tagliatelle. So, when Vincenzo Vernocchi, a talented winemaker, got in touch saying his nonna makes amazing *tagliatelle al ragù*, we jumped at the chance to visit her.

Alba greeted us wearing a deep blue, subtly brocaded dress and Versace trainers, drop earrings and a turquoise necklace. She has always been interested in fashion; her first job was working in tailor's shop, like so many young women of her age. And at 86 years old she is a fab example of comfy chic.

Alba's career in fashion didn't come to pass as she got married at 16 and, to begin with, worked with her husband on his farm. They ran an agriturismo, serving food, which became so successful that they left farming behind to concentrate on the restaurant, just outside Cesena, a town close to the Adriatic coast.

While making this dish, Alba shared several suggestions: first, like most cooks in the area she uses milk in the ragù, as it adds a touch of creaminess and sweetness and also balances out the acidity of the tomatoes. Next, she recommends using a tin of whole tomatoes and blitzing them to make a passata (sieved tomatoes) – the producers have to use their undamaged, unblemished tomatoes for this, making it a better-quality product. As for your pasta, if it's a little bit soft, then sprinkle grated Parmigiano over the sfoglia to stop it from sticking when you roll it up. Alba doesn't like too much surface flour on her pasta.

There is, in fact, an official recipe for *tagliatelle alla bolognese* that was registered with the Bologna Chamber of Commerce in 1972. This instructs cooks to add a half glass of red wine; Alba doesn't, but it's certainly an option, so have included it in this recipe. Ingredients can vary slightly, but long slow cooking is the key to a good ragù.

Recipe method overleaf

If you find it's a little bit soft, then sprinkle coarsely grated Parmigiano Reggiano over the sfoglia to stop it sticking when you roll it up.

FOR THE PASTA

400 g (14 oz/3⅓ cups) 00 flour or plain
   (all-purpose) flour
4 eggs

FOR THE RAGÙ

150 g (5 oz) unsmoked pancetta, minced
1 carrot, finely diced
1 celery stick, finely diced
1 onion, finely diced
200 g (7 oz) ground beef steak
200 g (7 oz) pork mince
a glass red wine (optional, about 125 ml/
   4 fl oz/½ cup)
400 g (14 oz) good-quality tin whole
   tomatoes (e.g. San Marzano or cherry)
1 tablespoon tomato purée
150 ml (5 fl oz/scant ⅔ cup) whole milk
1 bay leaf
freshly grated nutmeg (to taste)
salt

TO SERVE

grated Parmigiano Reggiano

Make the pasta as described on page 18. Once you have made your sfoglia, leave it for 5 minutes to dry a little, before rolling it up like a carpet and cutting across the pasta to create folded over ribbons about 7 mm (¾ in) wide. If you want to make nests, for easier handling, then take 4 rolled ribbons at a time, shake them out, drape them over a finger and grab the 8 ends. Keep holding them and wrap the strands around your hand so you end up with a nest and the ends are on the inside. This way, the ends don't dry out as quickly.

Take a casserole or deep sauté pan and heat it over a medium flame. Add the pancetta and fry it so the fat is released. Sauté the carrot, celery and onion, until the mixture is soft – it will take around 10 minutes. Then add the rest of the meat. Brown it, stirring frequently until the meat has broken up and looks like it's abandoned all hope of becoming a burger. If you want to add wine, do so now and let it evaporate. Blitz the tomatoes with a hand-held blender and pour this into the meat mixture. Stir in the tomato purée, half the milk, the bay leaf and plenty of freshly grated nutmeg. Let the mixture simmer very gently, adding more milk when necessary, for a couple of hours. At the end, when you push a spoon through the ragù you should briefly see the bottom of the pan.

Bring a large pan of water to the boil, add a generous couple of teaspoons of salt and return the water to the boil before heaping in your pasta. Give it a stir and test your pasta for doneness after 1 minute. It should have cooked within 2 minutes. Drain it, return it in the pan and stir through the ragù. You want the ragù to coat the pasta; resist the urge to drown your tagliatelle in the sauce.

Plate up and add a final flurry of Parmigiano Reggiano over each serving.

TONINA'S GARGANELLI PASTA WITH 'GYPSY' SAUCE

———

FOR 4-5 PEOPLE

Tonina is a whizz at *garganelli*. She helps with the local pasta *sagra* – their food festival – and is used to making pasta for hundreds of people.

Garganelli are meant to look like trachea – the tube connecting your nose to your lungs. They are the handmade equivalent of penne pasta, so swap them in this recipe and you have a very quick midweek supper. Tonina recommends you buy better quality green olives with the stone in and remove the stones yourself. Also, make sure your olives haven't been dyed – the clue is if they are bright green, they have been chemically treated and the taste will be inferior.

Traditionally, garganelli were made by rolling them along the piece of a weaving loom called a *pettine* in Italian – a comb. You will only find fragments for sale in antique markets and on line, and an acceptable substitute is a ridged cavatelli paddle. The grooves it makes aren't quite as fine as with a pettine, but the pasta still looks pretty and it tastes the same.

FOR THE PASTA
400g (14 oz/3⅓ cups) 00 flour or
    plain (all-purpose) flour
4 eggs

FOR THE 'GYPSY' SAUCE
200 g (7 oz) pancetta
1 onion, finely chopped
150 g (5 oz) sliced mushrooms
50 g (2 oz) green olives (destoned
    weight)
400 g (14 oz) passata (sieved tomatoes)
a knife tip of peperoncino or cayenne
    pepper
salt

TO SERVE
grated Parmigiano Reggiano (optional)

It's easier to deal with a twenty-egg dough than an amount just for two people.

Make the pasta as described on page 18. Roll the dough out into a sfoglia, and cut it into 5 cm (2 in) squares. Arrange each square on your cavatelli paddle so it is a diamond. Place the rod just below the corner closest to you, then flip the corner over the rod. Press your hands on either end of the rod and roll the pasta along the paddle, making sure the tube has sealed properly by pressing down when the tip furthest from you is underneath. It's not difficult but many hands make light work!

Chop the pancetta into little cubes – less than 1 cm (½ in), ideally – and then fry them in a sauté pan until some of the fat has been released. Add the onion and continue frying for about 5 minutes, until softened. Add the mushrooms, olives, passata and peperoncino or cayenne pepper, and let everything simmer for around 20 minutes. Taste the sauce after 10 minutes and see if you think it needs salt – it will depend on your olives.

Bring a large pan of salted water to the boil. Add your garganelli, let it come back to the boil and then cook for 3–5 minutes. How long they need will depend on how thick you have made them. Taste-test some to check for doneness – they should still be a bit chewy.

Drain the pasta and toss with the sauce. It's ready to be plated out with a sprinkling of Parmigiano Reggiano, if using.

PATRIZIA'S LASAGNA AL FORNO FROM TARANTO

FOR 4–6 PEOPLE

I was invited to film a friendly lasagne-making competition in Turin. It was one of the initiatives put on by a project called *Essere Anziani a Mirafiori Sud* – To be Elderly in South Mirafiori (a suburb of Turin) – based in a social centre on the edge of a park surrounded by high-rise flats. It organised 20 women into four teams, each trying to produce a three-course meal in one kitchen, while being very good natured about it all. Patrizia, like all the other participants, was originally from somewhere else in Italy, but had been attracted by the better work opportunities of Turin. She doesn't go back to Taranto in Puglia: 'These days, all my family is here,' she shrugged.

Patrizia was apologetic she hadn't made her lasagna sheets herself. 'I spent yesterday looking after my grandchildren,' she said a little sheepishly. Which is a very good reason to use a couple of packets, if you are short of time – but don't use the 'no need to pre-cook' kind of lasagna for this dish. It is a typical dish of Puglia, originally made as a way of using up leftovers, but nowadays the exuberant mixture of ingredients and labour-intensive meatballs all say 'it's party time'.

Incidentally, an Italian chef, Mauro Uliassi, recommended to me to use rice bran oil for frying; it's flavourless, has a high smoke point and is widely available these days in Italy.

Recipe photo overleaf

FOR THE PASTA

300 g (10½ oz/scant 2½ cups) finely
    ground semolina flour
150 ml (5 fl oz/⅔ cup) tepid water

FOR THE MEATBALLS

250 g (9 oz) minced veal (or beef)
150 g (5 oz) ground pork (or you could
    use top-quality sausage meat)
1 tablespoon chopped parsley
30 g (1 oz) grated Pecorino or
    Parmigiano Reggiano
rice bran or vegetable oil, for frying
150 g (5 oz) ground beef

FOR THE TOMATO SAUCE

4 tablespoons extra-virgin olive oil
1 onion, chopped
1 garlic, minced
1 carrot, diced
1 celery stick, diced
50 g (2 oz) ground beef (this is to give the
    tomato sauce more depth of flavour)
1 tablespoon chopped rosemary
1 teaspoon salt
2 × 400 g (14 oz) tins whole tomatoes

TO ASSEMBLE THE DISH

250 g (9 oz) cooked ham, thinly sliced
    and shredded into ribbons
3 × 150 g (5 oz) mozzarella balls, cubed
3 eggs, beaten
50 g (2 oz) Pecorino, grated, plus more
    to finish

This lasagna has three different components and
you can order them how you want. Here, I suggest
you make the pasta while the sauce is bubbling away.

For the meatballs, pulse together the veal, pork,
parsley and cheese in a blender. Chill the mixture for
30 minutes, so it's not so sticky.

Wet your hands and roll the mixture into equal-sized
balls – aim for them to be hazelnut- or marble-sized.
This quantity makes around 50 marble-sized meatballs.

Pour enough oil into a large frying pan (skillet) to
cover the base and heat until it is starting to shimmer
a bit. Fry your meatballs in batches – if you
overcrowd the pan, they will steam rather than
brown. Once browned, drain your meatballs on
kitchen paper to await the lasagna assembly. Fry the
remaining ground beef and put to one side.

To make the tomato sauce, heat the olive oil in a
large saucepan and cook the onion, garlic, carrot and
celery until softened. Add the ground beef and
brown it over a medium heat. Stir in the rosemary,
season with the salt and add the tomatoes, breaking
them up using the back of a spoon. Fill the tomato
tins with water add that too, then leave to simmer for
about 40 minutes, until the sauce has reduced and
thickened. Taste and adjust the seasoning at the end.

Make the pasta dough according to the
instructions on page 21. Roll it out as thinly as
possible – aim for about 2 mm – and cut it into
rectangles about one-third the size of your lasagna
dish, which should be about 30 × 40 cm (12 × 16 in)
and have deep sides.

Bring a large pan of salted water to the boil and
have a bowl or pot of cold water on standby. Cook
the pasta sheets a couple at a time for 3 minutes,
then dunk them in the cold water for couple of
minutes. When they are cool enough to handle,
spread them out on tea towels to drain.

When the sauce is ready, preheat the oven to
180°C (350°F/gas 4).

To assemble, spread a tablespoon of tomato sauce
across the bottom of your lasagna dish. Now add a
layer of pasta, making sure they don't overlap (trim
them if necessary), followed by a mixture of the
meatballs, the cooked ground beef, some ham,
mozzarella, beaten egg, Pecorino and more tomato
sauce. Repeat the layers twice more – or until you
have used up all the ingredients (the number of
layers will be determined by the size and shape of
your dish – if your dish is larger, then you will have
fewer layers).

Scatter over some grated Pecorino to finish. Cover
with foil and bake for 45 minutes. Let the lasagna
cool for 15 minutes before serving.

ANGELINA'S PAPPARELLE WITH LIVER

FOR 4-6 PEOPLE

Luca Dusi is one of those guys who sweeps you along with his enthusiasm for natural wine (which he imports), for life, for everything. So, when I asked him if he knew of any Pasta Grannies in the Verona area where he's from, he roared 'not a problem!' And a few weeks later we all piled into his mum Angelina's house for Sunday lunch. It was one of those hot July days where the only creatures moving were honey bees, and the kittens were stretched out under foliage, eventually roused by wafts of livers simmering on the stove.

Angelina wasn't bothered by the heat or the strangers with cameras in their hands. She set about making the typical Sunday lunch of Verona. *Papparelle* is not a typo; this pasta is very finely cut ribbons that are thinner than tagliolini. Think angel hair pasta. And they are served in a meat broth with a garnish of sautéed chicken livers, called *fegadina* in Veronese dialect.

FOR THE PASTA
400 g (14 oz/3⅓ cups) 00 flour
    or plain (all-purpose) flour
4 eggs

FOR THE BROTH
make the meat stock on page 203, but
    also add 6 juniper berries and 3 cloves

FOR THE FEGADINI
knob of butter
1 tablespoon extra-virgin olive oil
1 small white onion, finely diced
250 g (9 oz) cleaned, chopped chicken
    livers (in a more rustic version you
    can also add chicken hearts)
½ glass of dry white (Luca says,
    the other half is for the chef)
1 bay leaf
½ tablespoon finely chopped rosemary
salt

If you have an earthenware pot, add the butter, oil, onion and livers and place the pot over a very gentle heat. Once it is bubbling, add the wine and herbs. Season with salt and let it cook for 20 minutes.

If you are using an ordinary sauté pan, then heat it over a gentle heat, melt the butter in the oil and add the onion. Let the onion turn pale gold without burning, then add the chicken livers. Turn up the heat a little and stir them about with a wooden spoon, giving them a bit of colour. Next pour in the wine and stir through the herbs. Cook for 20 minutes and check for seasoning.

If you have added hearts, your stew is going to need to cook for another 15 minutes or so. Add a little of the broth to stop the meat from drying out.

Make the pasta as described on page 18. Roll up your sfoglia like a carpet then cut across the pasta as thinly as possible to create very fine ribbons. Shake out the ribbons and keep them spread out while you cut the rest.

Bring the stock to a simmer in a large saucepan and shovel in the papparelle. They will cook in about 1 minute. Angelina says, 'how much broth you serve is up to you. Some people plate up the pasta without any broth at all. I like a little bit.'

Strain the livers of any juice and remove the bay leaf. Plate up the pasta and add the livers to the middle of each serving.

Another tip from Angelina is that if you have any leftover livers, keep the juices, add a little more butter and blitz them to make a pâté, which is excellent on crostini for Sunday supper.

Angelina recommends you cook the livers in an earthenware pot. She says, 'Start cooking the livers from cold, this way they are more tender.'

BENEDETTO'S PAPPARDELLE WITH WILD BOAR RAGÙ

FOR 4 PEOPLE

I love it when we find a Pasta Grandpa. With the over 65s, cooking was (and still is) seen as women's work, so it's rare to find an older man who has taken up pasta making. Benedetto is one example. His grandmother from Ferrara taught him how to cook, but his career was as an agronomist. Nowadays, in his retirement, he cooks evening meals for his local butcher-cum-wine-bar and restaurant, Macelleria Lo Scalco in San Miniato, Tuscany.

Although wild boar is widespread across Italy, one doesn't often see it being sold in butchers, but this excellent shop is one of the places where you can buy it. And, of course, eat Benedetto's *pappardelle* with wild boar ragù.

Benedetto says you should freeze the meat for a couple of days if it is from a wild animal, as this helps to tenderise it. You could also use venison instead of boar, but note that your cooking times will be less.

FOR THE PASTA
400 g (14 oz/3⅓ cups) 00 flour
    or plain (all-purpose) flour
4 eggs

FOR THE MARINADED BOAR
600 g (1 lb 5 oz) boar steak
1 teaspoon black peppercorns, crushed
1 bay leaf
1 bottle red wine, or enough to cover
    the meat (drink the rest)

FOR THE RAGÙ
1 onion, diced
1 carrot, diced
1 celery stick, diced
1 garlic clove, finely chopped
4 tablespoons extra-virgin olive oil
2 thick rashers pancetta, diced
½ teaspoon ground cinnamon
½ teaspoon ground nutmeg
a pinch of cayenne pepper
1 square 80 per cent dark chocolate,
    grated
about 500 ml (17 fl oz/2 cups) red wine
salt
3 sage leaves, finely chopped
20 cm (8 in) sprig of rosemary, leaves
    stripped, finely chopped

TO SERVE
grated Parmigiano Reggiano

Cut the boar into small cubes, removing any gristle. Place it in a plastic bowl with the peppercorns and bay leaf and pour over the red wine. Cover and leave the meat to marinate in the fridge for 12 hours.

Drain the boar and discard the marinade. To make the ragù, sauté the onion, carrot, celery and garlic in olive oil with the pancetta in a large pan. Once the vegetables are soft, stir in the drained boar and season with the spices and the chocolate (it will add richness to the sauce).

Add enough red wine to cover the meat, season with salt, cover, and leave to simmer for a couple of hours; how long will depend on how mature the animal was. Add water or stock if it gets too dry – you want a small amount of liquid at the end, with tender, non-chewy, meat.

While it is cooking, make the pasta according to page 18. Pappardelle ribbons should be the width of your thumb (2–3 cm/¾–1 in).

When ready to serve, bring a large pan of salted water to the boil for the pasta and warm some serving bowls.

Add the chopped sage and rosemary into the ragù and give everything a good stir.

Chuck the pappardelle into boiling water and simmer the pasta for 2 minutes, then test them for doneness. Keeping back a ladle of pasta water, drain the pappardelle.

Toss the pappardelle and ragù – and the pasta water, if necessary – together. Plate the pasta up into the warmed bowls and sprinkle with a generous amount of grated Parmigiano Reggiano.

IDA'S TAJARIN WITH ROAST MEAT GRAVY

FOR 4 PEOPLE

Tajarin is the Piedmont version of tagliolini. You will often find recipes stipulating a large number of egg yolks, but this extravagance is for gastronomes and chefs, not frugal housewives. This pasta is often dressed with chicken or rabbit offal that has stewed for a couple of hours, but Ida's preferred sauce is the juices from a meat roast. If you have any leftover gravy, use it with this pasta. She likes to stir in a little more butter for extra richness (showing the French influence on cooking in this part of Italy). When we visited Ida, she used the pan juices from braising a mixture of pork, rose veal and rabbit, which was destined for her *agnolotti del plin* (see page 240). So here you can do a two-pasta festa!

FOR THE PASTA
400 g (14 oz/3⅓ cups) 00 flour
    or plain (all-purpose) flour
4 eggs
semolina flour, for dusting

FOR THE GRAVY
200 g (7 oz) pork loin
200 g (7 oz) rose veal stewing steak
200 g (7 oz) rabbit meat or boneless
    chicken thighs
1 tablespoon butter, plus extra for gravy
1 garlic clove
10 cm (4 in) sprig of rosemary
½ glass white wine (about 85 ml/
    2¾ fl oz/scant 5 tablespoons)
50 ml (1¾ fl oz/3 tablespoons) chicken
    stock (optional)

TO SERVE
grated Parmigiano Reggiano (preferably
    aged for 24 months)

Make the pasta dough as described on page 18. While it rests for 30 minutes, make the gravy.

Dice the meat into 2 cm (¾ in) pieces. Melt the butter in a sauté pan, and add the garlic clove, rosemary and the meat. Fry everything for a few minutes, so the meat turns white, then add the wine. Let this bubble for a minute or so and once you can

stop smelling alcohol, cover the pan with a lid and continue cooking the meat for around 15 minutes. If the juices in the pan dry out, add a splash of stock. Once the meat is cooked through (you can check by slicing a piece in half), remove the meat (reserve this for Ida's agnolotti recipe on page 240), garlic and rosemary. You should have some juices in the bottom of the pan. Add in a little more butter for extra richness and to make a thicker gravy – keep the it warm while you make the tajarin.

Divide the dough in half if your board is small. Roll out the pasta dough as thinly as possible, so you can see your hand through it. Sprinkle semolina over the surface and roll it up like a carpet. Use a straight-bladed, very sharp knife to slice across the roll to create very fine folded over ribbons, 2 mm wide. Shake them out, then spread the strands over the board so they don't stick together.

Bring a large pan of salted water to the boil. Heap the pasta into the water, wait for it to come back the boil then cook it for 1 minute. Nibble a strand to test it if it is cooked; continue to simmer the pasta if necessary.

Drain the pasta and add it to the buttery gravy. Mix everything together and serve with grated cheese.

OPTIONAL
Ida also likes to add a couple of spoons of a tomato-ey, meat ragù (which she always has on standby) to the gravy to give it a bit more body.

SILVANA'S POTATO RAVIOLI FROM MUGELLO

———

MAKES AROUND 90 TORTELLI, ENOUGH FOR 6-8 PEOPLE

Tortelli di Mugello are a potato-filled ravioli from a town called Mugello, just to the north of Florence. They are double carb heaven! Seventy-eight-year-old Silvana describes herself as a housewife and doesn't think of the 20 years she has spent making tortelli for a local restaurant as a proper job – she makes over 2,500 of them every day, although the dough is made and rolled for her with a machine. The filling is with real potato not *fiocchi di patate* – dried potato flakes – which can appear in some commercially made examples. At home, of course, she does everything by hand.

Silvana says, 'It's important the potato is very well seasoned, otherwise the finished tortelli will taste bland.' Not everyone adds tomato sauce to the potato – some prefer it plain – but Silvana likes to make the filling as flavoursome as possible. It surprised us to learn, despite the enjoyment she takes in making these tortelli, she is not particularly interested in eating them. 'Oh, I only cook for others,' she said.

Beef is her preference, but her son-in-law is a hunter, so she made a ragù using wild boar. Other cooks in the Mugello area also like to make a rabbit or a mushroom sauce. The tortelli may be frozen; cook them straight from the freezer if so.

Recipe photo overleaf

FOR THE PASTA
400 g (14 oz/3⅓ cups) 00 flour
    or plain (all-purpose) flour
4 eggs
1 tablespoon extra-virgin olive oil

FOR THE TOMATO SAUCE
2 garlic cloves, minced
a handful of parsley, finely chopped
50 ml (1¾ fl oz/3 tablespoons) extra-
    virgin olive oil
250 g (9 oz) passata (sieved tomatoes)
salt and pepper

FOR THE FILLING
1.5 kg (3 lb 5 oz) old floury potatoes
    (unpeeled weight)
3 tablespoons grated Parmigiano
    Reggiano
freshly grated nutmeg (to taste)

FOR THE MEAT SAUCE
2 red onions, finely diced
1 small carrot, finely diced
1 celery stick, finely diced
1 tablespoon chopped parsley
3–4 tablespoons extra-virgin olive oil
500 g (1 lb 2 oz) ground beef steak or
    ground wild boar
400 g (14 oz) passata (sieved tomatoes)
salt and pepper

Make the dough as described on page 18, adding the oil along with the eggs. Silvana says the absolute minimum her dough should rest is 30 minutes – it's okay to leave it for longer.

For the tomato sauce, mix the garlic and parsley together. Heat the oil in a small saucepan and fry the mixture with a generous pinch of salt until the garlic is tender but not golden. Add the passata with a tablespoon of water and continue cooking for another 15 minutes or so, until the sauce has darkened and reduced. Adjust the seasoning with a little pepper and more salt if necessary. Set aside.

Boil the potatoes until tender, then remove their skins while they are still warm. Use a potato ricer to mash them. Stir through the cheese and half the tomato sauce (about 250 ml/8 fl oz/1 cup), turning the mash pink. Taste it; you should add enough tomato sauce to give it a savoury flavour. Add some more if necessary; any excess sauce can be added to the meat sauce. Season with some freshly grated nutmeg.

For the meat sauce, mix the diced vegetables with the chopped parsley. Silvana then starts frying this mixture for a good 10 minutes without any oil. Only when she thinks she has driven off most of the moisture in the vegetables does she add the olive oil and continues to sauté the mixture for another 15 minutes until everything is very soft. She was taught to make the *soffritto* this way by her mother. You may want to cook the soffritto in the usual way by softening it in oil in a casserole. Either way, the key is to cook it slowly for at least 25 minutes.

Crumble the minced meat into the vegetable pan, give it a good stir and continue to fry for another 20 minutes or so, until the meat is properly browned and looks like a fine rubble. Add the passata, season generously with salt and pepper, and pour in 500 ml (17 fl oz/2 cups) water. Let this simmer away gently, covered, for 2 hours.

Meanwhile, make the tortelli. With this amount of dough, you may want to roll it out in two batches. Cut the pasta sheet into strips 12 cm (5 in) wide. Roll the mashed potato into walnut-sized balls and place them 5 cm (2 in) apart along the middle of the pasta strips. Fold the pasta over the line of potato balls and press down around each ball to remove the air from within each tortello. Take a fluted pastry cutter and cut equidistant between each mound. Trim the cut edges with the cutter and then press down around the filling with the prongs of a fork to ensure the edges are properly sealed. Place on a tray or on the table. They can be left like this for a couple of hours before cooking.

Once the ragù has cooked and reduced to a thick sauce, bring a large saucepan of salted water to the boil. Warm a serving platter. For this amount of tortelli you will need to cook them in batches. Add some of the tortelli and once the water has returned to the boil, cook for 4 minutes. Scoop them out with a slotted spoon or sieve and lay them on the warmed platter. Dress with some ragù and repeat until they are all cooked and annointed with meat sauce.

Locals do not add cheese to the finished dish.

DORIANA'S FARRO TAGLIOLINI WITH PANCETTA

———

FOR 4 PEOPLE

~~~~~~~~~~~~~~~~~~~~~

Doriana runs an agriturismo called Il Cerreto in Umbria, central Italy. She rears her own black pigs and the pancetta made from them has lovely firm and flavoursome fat. Try and get hold of the best-quality pancetta or bacon for this recipe, it will make all the difference to the flavour.

Farro, known as emmer in the US, is an ancient wheat. It is not the same variety as spelt, which is more commonly found in the UK and which has a rounder grain and is a little softer than farro when it's cooked, but the flours can be used interchangeably. Doriana says you cannot roll the pasta as thinly as you can when using 00 white flour, and you should let the sfoglia dry for 10 minutes or so, otherwise the tagliolini (thin tagliatelle) will be difficult to cut.

FOR THE PASTA
300 g (10½ oz/2½ cups) farro flour
100 g (3½ oz) 00 flour or plain
    (all-purpose) flour
4 eggs

FOR THE PANCETTA
2 tablespoons extra-virgin olive oil
4 thick rashers of pancetta
1 onion, diced
1 red chilli, seeds removed (or not –
    how fiery you want it is up to you)
a glass of white wine (125 ml/4 fl oz/
    ½ cup)
400 g (14 oz) tin chopped tomatoes
    (or fresh if it is the height of summer)
25 g (¾ oz) grated Pecorino Romano,
    plus extra for serving
salt

Make the pasta dough as described on page 18. Leave your sfoglia to dry while you make the sauce.

Heat the oil in a sauté pan. Slice your pancetta into matchsticks and fry them briskly until the fat has been released from the meat, and it's starting to colour. Remove the pancetta from the pan, leaving the fat behind, and put it to one side.

Fry the onion and chilli in the oil over a medium heat until the onion is soft. This will take around 7 minutes. Deglaze the pan with the wine and keep frying while the alcohol evaporates. The steam from the pan should cease to smell winey. Add the tomatoes and the pancetta, and give everything a good stir. Season with a pinch of salt. Let it bubble away while you slice your pasta.

Smooth your sfoglia with a little 00 flour. Roll it up like a carpet and with a cleaver or straight-bladed knife (which you have sharpened), slice across as thinly as possible to create fine ribbons. Unroll the ribbons and toss them with your hands to give them a good airing. Keep the ribbons spread out to stop them from sticking.

Bring a pan of salted water to a spirited boil, and heap your pasta into the water. The tagliolini will cook quickly in about 2 minutes.

Remove the chilli from the sauce. Scoop the pasta out of the pan with a slotted spoon or sieve and ladle it into the sauté pan. Add the grated Pecorino Romano and toss everything together. Plate up immediately, sprinkling with more cheese if you wish.

EMILIA'S 'GUITAR' SPAGHETTI WITH TINY MEATBALLS

FOR 4-6 PEOPLE

My husband and I were enjoying a few days exploring the wine regions of Abruzzo, when Alessia and her husband Fabrizio from Maple and Saffron tours contacted me about Fabrizio's nonna, Emilia. 'She can make *spaghetti alla chitarra con pallottine,*' they said, so, of course, this was too big a temptation. I found myself meeting Emilia – with my husband and friends in tow.

Emilia started cooking pasta for her family when she was about 10 years old. Pasta and beans was a family favourite. *Spaghetti alla chitarra con pallottine* was, and still is, a dish served up on high days and holiday – Emilia has made huge quantities for weddings over the years. A dish that gave her particular pleasure as a child was polenta and sausages. The polenta would be poured directly onto the table and the family would tuck in with their forks. This harks back to the days when folk could not afford crockery – and would have eaten the polenta with their fingers.

The day we met was extremely hot. Emilia says on days like this, you may need to add an extra egg to your dough to keep it pliable and soft.

To make the pasta, you will need a *chitarra,* which means guitar in Italian, which can be bought on the internet for around £30 ($40). Or you may have a spaghetti cutter attachment for your pasta maker. The cheapest financial outlay is a grooved spaghetti rolling pin.

Emilia likes to use a grade 1 flour, which is difficult to find outside Italy. It's about 9.5 per cent gluten and the '1' refers to the relatively coarse grind. If you cannot track some down, then I suggest using your usual pasta flour mixed with 10 per cent stoneground wholemeal flour.

Recipe photo overleaf

FOR THE PASTA

400 g (14 oz/3⅓ cups) soft wheat flour,
    grade 1 (see introduction)
4 eggs
1 tablespoon extra-virgin olive oil
2 g (½ teaspoon) salt

FOR THE TOMATO SAUCE

4 tablespoons extra-virgin olive oil
1 celery stick, cut in half
2 carrots, halved
3 garlic cloves
100 g (3½ oz) slice of braising steak
    or veal
3 pork ribs
100 ml (3½ fl oz) white wine
1 teaspoon salt
1.5 kg (3 lb 5 oz) skinned, chopped
    fresh tomatoes (or very good-quality
    bottled tomatoes)

FOR THE MEATBALLS

500 g (1 lb 2 oz) finely ground beef
1 egg, beaten
½ teaspoon salt
1 tablespoon extra-virgin olive oil
a pinch of freshly ground black pepper
nutmeg, freshly grated (to taste)
1 tablespoon grated Pecorino, plus extra
    to serve (optional)
extra-virgin olive oil, to fry the meatballs

First make the tomato sauce. Heat the oil in a casserole or heavy-bottomed saucepan and sauté the celery, carrots and garlic for 5 minutes. Add the meat and cook the pieces until golden. Deglaze the pan with the wine and let it reduce so you can no longer smell the alcohol evaporating. Remove the garlic, and add the salt and tomatoes. Cover with a lid and cook the sauce for at least 3 hours over a very low heat, stirring every so often when needed. You may need to add a little water from time to time, but you are aiming for a thick sauce. Once it is cooked, strip the meat from the ribs and chop up the steak, then return the meat to the tomato sauce. Discard the bones and the whole vegetables.

For the meatballs, mix everything together in a bowl – make sure it's a good mush! Then wet your hands and roll chickpea-sized meatballs. This takes ages, so try and get the whole family involved. Fry them in batches, in olive oil, until they are just cooked – it will only take a few minutes. Give the pan a good shake and stir them with a spatula so they brown on all sides and don't stick to the pan. Place them on kitchen paper while you cook the rest. Drain off any excess oil at the end.

Mix the tomato sauce with the meatballs, but reserve a few meatballs to scatter over each serving. This mixture can now be put to one side and kept warm – or chill it for future use. It will keep in the fridge for a couple of days.

To make the pasta, mix the ingredients together and knead the dough until it is smooth and homogenous. It will take about 10 minutes. Cover the dough and leave it to rest for at least 30 minutes. Roll it out into a sfoglia which is about 3 mm thick.

Cut the dough into broad slices which fit your chitarra and lay one at a time along the narrow set of strings. Using a rolling pin, push hard down and along the pasta (see photo overleaf). You may need to strum the strings to loosen the pasta strands. Keep them well floured while you work your way through the dough strips.

Make sure the tomato and meatball mixture is hot and bring a large pan of salted water to the boil. Cook the spaghetti strands for 5 minutes or so.

To serve, layer the pasta with the sauce, sprinkle the reserved meatballs over, along with some grated Pecorino, if you like.

VIOLETTA'S MACCHERONI WITH KID RAGÙ

FOR 4 PEOPLE

If Italy is a boot, then Basilicata is in the arch of the foot. It's a mountainous region where ghost-grey Podolica cattle roam without fences, munching their way through leathery herbs with huge bells hanging off their collars. They are adapted to the harsh terrain, as are goats. One doesn't think of goat meat featuring in Italian cooking, but it does. We visited Violetta in the medieval village of Sant'Arcangelo, whose streets are a donkey-cart wide. They are no longer in evidence, but there are plenty of traditional tools and habits that still flourish.

Violetta likes to make her maccheroni using a twig from a Genista – a broom shrub. It's called *cannicell'* in dialect and her recipe *maccheroni a cannicell' col sugo di capretto*, directly translates as 'macaroni hand-rolled with a little cane with a kid-goat sauce'. Twigs from the Genista plant are straight and have a rough, ridged surface which helps stop the pasta from sticking. This foraged piece of pasta kit predates the *ferro* or square-sided metal rod, which door-to-door salesmen used to sell to housewives in this part of the world.

FOR THE PASTA
400 g (14 oz/3⅓ cups) finely ground semolina flour
2 g (½ teaspoon) salt
180–200 ml (6–7 fl oz/¾–scant 1 cup) warm water

FOR THE KID RAGÙ
4 tablespoons extra-virgin olive oil
1 garlic clove, chopped
600 g (1 lb 7 oz) cubed kid-goat or lamb steaks from the leg
small bunch of parsley, chopped
4 large fresh ripe tomatoes, skinned and chopped
400 g (14 oz) passata (sieved tomatoes)
salt

Make the pasta as described on page 21. While it rests, cook the meat sauce.

Heat the oil in a sauté pan over a moderate heat. Fry the garlic for about a minute – don't let it burn – before adding the cubed kid steak, parsley and fresh tomato and passata. Violetta thinks this mix of fresh tomatoes and homemade passata gives optimal flavour. Season with salt according to your taste

buds. Cover with a lid. This ragù only needs to simmer for about 30–40 minutes as kid is so tender. Add a little water if it looks like it's going to dry out too much during cooking.

To make the pasta, pull pieces of dough off the main lump and roll it out into a rope about the thickness of a pencil. Snip it into 10 cm (4 in) lengths. To make a tube of maccheroni, place your rod at a slight angle along the pasta, so that when you roll with your palm flat across the *ferro*, the pasta twists around it to create the tube. It takes practise and it doesn't matter if the maccheroni has holes along its seam. Keep going until you have rolled all your dough. Make sure your maccheroni is spread out and not lying on top of one another.

Bring salted water to a boil in a large saucepan and slide your pasta into it. Simmer for a couple of minutes and taste one. It might need a minute or two longer.

Violetta doesn't drain her pasta water down the sink. She puts the plug in and keeps the water for rinsing her plates. This is what frugal housewives used to do when running water wasn't a given.

You now have a choice – either toss the pasta and sauce together, or remove the kid-goat and serve this as a main course, mixing only the tomato sauce with the maccheroni.

LUCIA'S RASCHIATELLI WITH SALAMI AND HORSERADISH

———

FOR 4 PEOPLE

Eighty-nine-year-old Lucia had come out of hospital the day before we took this photo. She had returned to working in her family's bakery immediately. 'Shouldn't you rest just a little?', we wondered. 'This is my life,' she answered. 'What would I do at home? I have worked here in this bakery for over 60 years.' Lucia's son and grandson now manage the business but they continue to buy their durum wheat flour from a mill in nearby Matera, just like Lucia and her husband did. The bread is crusty, chewy and decidedly more-ish. There is a steady stream of people dropping by to pick some up – it's a Monday and the loaf will last a week. Lucia gestured to them. 'The village has changed – young people have to leave to find work. I like it best in the summer when everyone comes home.'

In this recipe, Lucia uses a local *lucanica* salami (this means it's from Basilicata). The meat had been chopped, not minced, so there are nice chunks of meat, coarsely crushed peppercorns and a reasonable marbling of fat. Take yourself off to your nearest Italian deli and cross examine the manager about his or her range. *Capocollo* (cured meat from the neck) would make a good substitute. Make sure to buy it in one slab, rather than thin slices. You want nuggets, not shreds of salami in your sugo.

The other unusual ingredient in this dish is horseradish – something you don't come across in other regions of Italy, except in the far north where there is German and Austrian influence on cooking. One theory is that the plant was introduced by Albanian immigrants several centuries ago. One can now buy fresh horseradish but wear glasses to peel the skin and then blitz it in a food processor, which is less pungent on the eyes than using a handheld grater. This dish is typically served in winter.

Recipe method overleaf

FOR THE PASTA

400 g (14 oz/3⅓ cups) finely ground
    semolina flour
200 ml (7 fl oz/scant 1 cup) tepid water
2 g (½ teaspoon) salt

FOR THE SALAMI SAUCE

2 tablespoons extra-virgin olive oil
1 garlic clove
400 g (14 oz) tin chopped tomatoes
salt
350 g (12 oz) salami, e.g. lucanica,
    capocollo or finocchietto, diced

TO SERVE

2 tablespoons freshly grated horseradish
    (or to taste)
plenty of grated Pecorino

Make the pasta dough as described on page 21. Lucia makes three-fingered raschiatelli for this dish. To do this, cut off a lump of dough and roll it out to around the thickness of your forefinger (unless it's very large). Slice it into lengths which approximate to your middle three digits. Press down with those fingers into a piece of dough and pull it towards you to make a concave, mini-trough of pasta. Repeat these steps until you've used up all your dough.

To make the sauce, heat the oil in a saucepan and add the garlic clove. Let it sizzle for 2 minutes before adding the tomatoes. Season with a little salt and let everything simmer for about 10 minutes to make a thickish sauce before adding the diced salami. Continue cooking the sauce to warm the salami through – it doesn't need lots of cooking. Remove the garlic clove.

Bring a large saucepan of salted water to the boil and add the pasta. Once the *raschiatelli* have bobbed to the surface, nibble one to test for doneness and cook for a little longer, if necessary.

Drain the pasta and toss with the sauce. Plate up with a scattering of both horseradish and cheese.

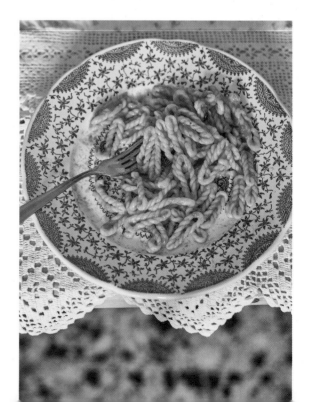

CESARIA'S LORIGHITTAS WITH CHICKEN

———

FOR 4 PEOPLE

Morgongiori is a little village on the western side of central Sardinia, and it is the only place on the island – and indeed the whole of Italy – where *lorighittas* are made. These double-hooped, twisted strands of thin, spaghetti-shaped pasta are made for eating on All Saints' Day, 1 November. In the days and centuries before radio, TV and mobile phones, making lorighittas was an opportunity for women to get together to gossip and sing. They would start production after the feast of Santa Sofia in mid-October and even today no-one has found a way to mechanise the process. Cesaria, who is 95, is able to roll fine strands even though, she says, the flour isn't the same as it used to be.

The traditional sauce for this pasta is made with a young rooster. Autumn was the season to dispatch cockerels that were surplus to requirements before they reached sexual maturity.

FOR THE PASTA
2 g (½ teaspoon) salt
200 ml (7 fl oz/scant 1 cup) warm water
400 g (14 oz/3⅓ cups) finely ground
 semolina flour

FOR THE CHICKEN SAUCE
3 tablespoons extra-virgin olive oil
1 onion
2 garlic cloves, minced
1.8 kg (4 lb) free-range, organic chicken,
 jointed into 8 pieces
50 ml (1¾ fl oz/3 tablespoons) white
 wine
750 g (1 lb 10 oz) passata (sieved
 tomatoes)
20 g (¾ oz) parsley, chopped
salt

TO SERVE
grated Pecorino Sardo

To make the pasta, dissolve the salt in the water and proceed according to the explanation on page 21. Some cooks like to add salt directly to the flour, but Cesaria likes to pat salted water onto the dough if it's too dry. Cesaria advises not to try to make this pasta when the weather is hot and dry.

Take small chunks of the dough and roll each one into a spaghetti strand 2.5 mm in diameter – getting the strand this thin takes a little bit of practise. Snip the strand into 20 cm (8 in) lengths and roll it twice round 3 fingers (if they are fairly small) and pinch the ends together. Pinch off any excess. Hold the loop at the join and twist it with the other hand like you are winding a watch; it helps to watch Cesaria's video on YouTube. Remember, this is a group activity so get family involved to work your way through the dough. The women of Morgongiori place the lorighittas on large flat baskets to dry – but a tea towel will do.

To make the chicken sauce, heat the oil in a casserole or Dutch oven and soften the onion for 5 minutes before stirring in the garlic. Cook the mixture for a minute or so more before adding the chicken pieces, wine and passata; there's no need to brown the chicken pieces first. Add a pinch of salt, cover with the lid and let everything simmer for a good 45 minutes. Add the parsley at the end of the cooking. Remove the chicken pieces; they can either be served alongside the pasta, or do as Sardinians do and serve it as a main course after the pasta.

Bring a large pan of salted water to the boil. Add the lorighittas and cook for about 8–10 minutes. Drain them and then dress them with the Pecorino and stir through the tomato sauce. The lorighittas are now ready to be eaten, with or without the chicken.

VANNA'S CICCIONEDDUS WITH LAMB RAGÚ

—

FOR 6–8 PEOPLE

Sardinia is home to several styles of gnocchi-shaped pasta, known collectively as *gnocchetti Sardi*. They come in different sizes and what they have in common is their textured surface made by rolling the pasta, most often along the base of beautiful flat baskets made from reeds. This creates grooves in the pasta to catch the sauce, and one doesn't find them anywhere else in Italy. So, unless you visit Sardinia and can track down a basket to buy, a gnocchi paddle is a reasonable substitute. *Ciccioneddus* are tiny gnocchetti Sardi made in the Sassari region of north-west Sardinia.

Vanna and her friends had decided to dress in traditional costume to honour the occasion: the men looked dashing in white pleated shirts and black hats, while the women wore corseted blouses, full length skirts and aprons.

The occasion was food as a theatrical production. There was music and friends who had come along; it was a party. Which is as it should be, because this recipe is traditionally served at weddings.

FOR THE PASTA
600 g (1 lb 5 oz) finely ground semolina
    flour
270–300 ml (9–10 fl oz/1¼ cups)
    tepid water
pinch of salt

FOR THE RAGÚ
4 tablespoons extra-virgin olive oil
1 onion, diced finely
500 g (1 lb 2 oz) lamb steak, diced
680 g (1 lb 8 oz) passata (sieved
    tomatoes)
2 bay leaves
1 sprig of rosemary
4 sprigs of thyme
4 sage leaves
8 basil leaves
1 teaspoon allspice, crushed
salt

TO SERVE
grated Pecorino Sardo

Make the pasta as described on page 21. Take a handful of dough and roll out a rope about 1 cm (½ in) thick. Then slice it up into pieces the size of an uncooked cannellini bean. Repeat until you have chopped up all the dough. Next, take a gnocchi paddle in one hand and roll each pasta nugget down the board with your thumb to create a C-shape. It's faster work if you get your family and friends involved, which Vanna did.

To make the ragù, heat a large saucepan on a medium heat and cover the bottom with oil. Add the onion and a pinch of salt and cook for 7–10 minutes, until translucent and soft. Add the lamb, browning the pieces on all sides.

Pour the passata into the pan, along with 100 ml (3½ fl oz/scant ½ cup) water (shaken around the bottle to remove all the tomato sauce). Add the herbs, the allspice and a half teaspoon of salt. Leave the lamb to simmer for 30 minutes with the lid on, then remove the lid and simmer for a further 10 minutes. Check the seasoning and remove all the herbs before serving.

Bring a large pan of salted water to the boil. Warm a serving platter. Add the ciccioneddus and simmer them for 5–6 minutes - nibble one to check they're cooked. Drain the pasta thoroughly and pour it onto the warmed platter. Mix in the ragù and scatter generous amounts of cheese over the top.

Eat with family and friends and toast everyone's good fortune.

LUCIA AND CATERINA'S PASTA WITH MEATBALLS

FOR 4 PEOPLE

Lucia and Caterina live in the village of Depressa in the Salento region of Puglia, and they have been best friends since they were little, seeing each other every day for over 75 years. They first came across each other in the church playgroup and have remained active members of the congregation. I asked why they were best of friends and they looked at each other and laughed. 'She's nice!', 'She makes me smile every time I see her!' 'Caterina made my wedding dress y'know,' Lucia said proudly. Both are grandmothers: Lucia has 12 grandchildren and Caterina has four. And this pasta recipe is one they serve their respective families for Sunday lunch. 'Everyone makes sagne on Sundays. Sometimes other people don't bother with the meatballs, they just make a meat ragù, but children love polpette,' said Caterina.

Sagne torte are twisted ribbons of pasta, which are also called *sagne ncannulate* in the local dialect. *Polpettine*, meanwhile, means little meatballs; polpette are ordinary sized ones; and *polpettone* means meat loaf. This same mixture can be used for all the sizes, though of course meat loaf and pasta would be a bit of a strange combination.

It helps to have meat which is finely ground – in Italy, the butcher will do this for you. If the meat you are using is coarsely minced, give it a pulse in a food processor.

FOR THE PASTA

400 g (14 oz/3⅓ cups) finely ground
    semolina flour
200 ml (7 fl oz/scant 1 cup) tepid water
a pinch of salt

FOR THE TOMATO SAUCE

3 tablespoons extra-virgin olive oil
1 onion, diced
1 garlic clove, crushed in a little salt
750 g (1 lb 10 oz) passata (sieved
    tomatoes)
3–4 stems of fresh basil
½ teaspoon chilli flakes (optional)
salt

FOR THE MEATBALLS

300 g (11 oz) ground pork
300 g (11 oz) ground beef
40 g (1½ oz) fine breadcrumbs
50 g (2 oz) grated hard Pecorino
    (or Parmigiano Reggiano, but
    that's not a Pugliese cheese)
2 tablespoons chopped parsley
2 tablespoons wine
1 egg, beaten
salt and pepper
freshly grated nutmeg (to taste)
vegetable oil, for frying

TO SERVE

grated Pecorino or ricotta salata

Make the pasta dough as described on page 21. Roll it out so the sfoglia is about 2 mm thick. Slice the pasta into 2 cm (¾ in) wide ribbons. Then hold on to one end of a ribbon while you use the palm of your other hand to roll the ribbon across the board. Turn it round and give the untwisted end another roll. Fold the ribbon in half if it is long and unwieldy and place it on a tea towel. Repeat until you have used all your dough. The sagne will keep like this for several hours.

To make the tomato sauce, heat the oil in a saucepan and sauté the onion until it is translucent. Stir in the garlic and cook the mixture for another minute before adding the passata and basil. Season with salt and add the chilli if you like. Leave the sauce to simmer gently for 30 minutes or so.

To make small meatballs, mix all the ingredients together (apart from the oil) and season with plenty of salt, pepper and nutmeg. Fry a teaspoon and taste it to check it is to your liking.

Wet your hands and roll marble-sized meatballs. Cover the bottom of a small frying pan (skillet) with a generous amount of vegetable oil and heat it until it shimmers. Add your meatballs, a few at a time, and brown them. Once nicely coloured (they do not have to be cooked all the way through), add them to the tomato sauce.

Continue to cook the tomato sauce and meatballs together for another 15 minutes or so. Check that the meatballs are cooked through but still juicy in the middle.

Bring a large pan of salted water to the boil, and add your sagne. Once the water has returned to the boil, cook for another 4 minutes. Drain the pasta and toss it with the meatballs. Serve with a generous scattering of grated cheese and toast the joys of lifelong friendships.

seven

Pasta
in brodo

Pastasciutta is an Italian word to describe pasta drained of its cooking liquid and dressed in a sauce of some kind. In this chapter, however, are examples of pasta in *brodo*, dishes which are both traditional and celebratory because of the time it takes to make them. First cooks prepare a stock with meat – which is served as the main course – and then the pasta is poached in the broth. In the Pulses chapter (see pages 86–107), you will find examples of pasta being cooked in a bean soup, which is another way of serving pasta in its cooking liquid. Note that these recipes all come from the north of Italy.

~~~~~~~~~~~~~~~~~~~~~~~~

MEAT STOCK

————

**MAKES 4 LITRES (1 GALLON),
ENOUGH FOR 8 PEOPLE**

~~~~~~~~~~~~~~~~~~~~~~~~

All the recipes in this chapter start with making a *brodo*, a meat stock. Of course, our Grannies' recipes all vary slightly, but they broadly follow this one – using a mixture of meat, including beef, chicken (sometimes capon), occasionally pork – and even lamb and mutton in Sardinia and Abruzzo. Italians like to simmer pieces of fresh meat – as opposed to previously roasted meat bones – to make a stock and then eat the meat as a separate main course. The stock is used for special occasion pasta, such as *tortellini* and *cappelletti*. The stock will also freeze well for up to three months.

about 1.5 kg (3 lb 5 oz) selection from
  chicken leg and wings, beef rib, beef
  neck, a piece of steak, like a skirt and/
  or pork shoulder
1 onion, quartered
2 celery sticks
1 carrot
1 bay leaf
6 peppercorns
some fresh tomatoes if it's summer,
  which add a pleasing colour
a good teaspoon of salt

Find yourself a stockpot which will hold about 4 litres (1 gallon) water. Add all the ingredients to it, then cover with enough water that it reaches 5 cm (2 in) or so below the rim of the pot. (I always add the salt at the beginning because I don't like the smell of unsalted boiling meat – salting makes the aromas savoury – but you may prefer to season the stock at the end of its cooking.) Cover with the lid and bring it to a gentle simmer. Let the stock burble quietly for a good 90 minutes, skimming off any scum that forms. Turn off the heat and let the meat cool in the stock. You can use the meat in ravioli fillings, or cover it in a salsa verde to make it interesting, the way Italians do.

Strain the stock of its solids and once it is room temperature, place it in the fridge overnight. Next day, skim off the fat which will have formed on the surface.

You can now use the stock or freeze it for later.

How much to serve will depend on the size of your soup bowl, but estimate 200 ml (7 fl oz/scant 1 cup) per bowl. You need more stock to cook the pasta in than you do to serve it. You can use the leftovers in other soups.

MARIA'S CAPPELLETTI IN MEAT STOCK

———

FOR 6 PEOPLE

Eighty-five-year-old Maria loves making pasta – she especially enjoys rolling it out. She uses semolina flour from one brand, De Cecco, and a pasta flour from another, Spadoni, to create the dough she likes for *cappelletti*. Cappelletti means 'little hats', and they have been made since medieval times. They used to be a Christmas Day treat, but now they are enjoyed all year round. Fillings vary across Emilia Romagna. In Faenza, it is a mixture of cheeses. Maria uses equal quantities of a local soft cheese called *bucciatello*, Parmigiano Reggiano and cow's milk ricotta. If you can't find the latter, swap it for any soft or semi-soft cheese that you can mash with a fork, such as robiola.

4 litres (1 gallon) meat stock
   (see page 203)

FOR THE PASTA
200 g (7 oz/1²/₃ cups) 00 flour or plain
   (all-purpose) flour
100 g (3½ oz) finely ground semolina
   flour
3 eggs

FOR THE FILLING
200 g (7 oz) grated Parmigiano Reggiano
   (preferably aged for 36 months)
200 g (7 oz) cow's milk ricotta, drained
   weight
200 g (7 oz) soft cheese, e.g. robiola
   or bucciatello (see introduction)
1 egg yolk
¼ teaspoon freshly grated nutmeg

TO SERVE
grated Parmigiano Reggiano

Make the pasta dough as described on page 18, leaving it to rest for at least an hour, or ideally overnight, before rolling.

Cut 5 cm (2 in) squares out of the dough, keeping the rest of the squares covered with a tea towel so the dough does not dry out while you make the cappelletti. Maria uses a special ravioli pasta cutter for this task, but a knife and a ruler work just as well.

To make the filling, mash all the cheeses with the egg yolk and nutmeg. Place a small, marble-sized piece of the mixture into the centre of each pasta square. Fold the pasta over the cheese nugget to create a right-angled triangle. Press and seal the edges of the triangle, then bring the two smaller-angled corners together around your finger to create a 'hat' and press them together firmly. Repeat until you have finished the mixture. This should be enough for about 70 cappelletti.

Warm some serving bowls and bring the stock to a simmer in a large saucepan. Cook the cappelletti gently in batches for 5 or so minutes – test one to see if they are done.

Ladle out the pasta with some of the stock onto plates and serve immediately. Pass around the grated Parmigiano Reggiano. You will have stock left over, but it can be used in other soups.

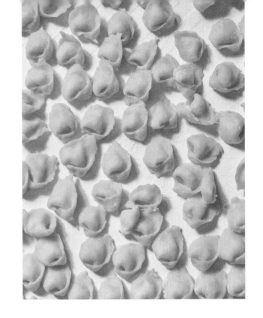

GISELLA'S 'SFOGLIA LORDA'

FOR 4–6 PEOPLE

Gisella lives in Faenza and this easy pasta originates from a little town just to the south of the city called Brisighella. *Sfoglia lorda* means dirty pasta in Italian, which gives you an idea of how generous you should be with the cheese filling. It was a way of using up excess filling originally intended for cappelletti – and for when cooks had had enough of folding them up!

You could use the same mixture as described in the previous recipe; however, Gisella uses a slightly different mixture of cheeses. She also includes one that is not available outside the Faenza area, called Campagnolo Romagnolo. As before, if you can get hold of robiola cheese instead, that would be a good substitute. You're looking for a tangy cheese, which is solid but still possible to mash with your fork.

4 litres (1 gallon) meat stock
  (see page 203)

FOR THE PASTA
300 g (10½ oz/2½ cups) 00 flour
  or plain (all-purpose) flour
50 g (2 oz) finely ground semolina flour
50 g (2 oz) wholemeal flour
4 eggs

FOR THE CHEESE FILLING
100 g (3½ oz) grated Parmigiano
  Reggiano (preferably aged for
  24 months)
150 g (5 oz) tangy soft cheese, such as
  robiola, or a soft, fresh goat's milk
  cheese
100 g (3½ oz) cow's milk ricotta, drained
1 large egg
¼ teaspoon freshly grated nutmeg
pinch of salt, to taste

TO SERVE
grated Parmigiano Reggiano

Make the pasta dough as described on page 18. Roll it out into a sheet thin enough that you can see your hand through it. Fold it in half, press the fold lightly, and then unfold it; you should have created a crease in the middle of the sfoglia.

Make the filling by mashing the cheeses together with the egg. Grate plenty of nutmeg into the mixture. Taste and season with salt. You should have a mushy, spreadable, but not lumpy or wet mixture. Use a spatula to smear this evenly and thinly over the half of the pasta sheet that is closest to you. Leave a 1 cm (½ in) border around the edge of the dough, then fold the un-cheesy half of the pasta sheet over the top. Pat it down to get the cheese to stick to the top pasta layer. Take a fork and stab it lightly all over, to stop any air bubbles from forming.

Use a fluted pastry cutter to make a grid of squares the size of postage stamps. You do not need to separate the squares before cooking them.

In a large pan, bring the stock to a gentle simmer. Use a wide spatula to lower the pasta squares gently into the pan. You may have to do this in batches. You want them to cook at a gentle waltz not a canter. When the squares bob to the surface, which will take 2–3 minutes, they're cooked. Taste one to check.

Ladle the pasta into soup bowls and scatter more Parmigiano Reggiano over the top. Eat immediately.

CRISTINA'S TORTELLINI IN BROTH

MAKES ABOUT 500 TORTELLINI,
ENOUGH FOR 12 SERVINGS

Cristina doesn't remember when she first started making pasta; she thinks she was about five years old. But it wasn't until she had retired from working on the production line of a cigarette factory that her love of pasta really took off. These days, she makes tortellini for family, friends, and friends of friends, using her grandmother's recipe. Her husband, Gianni, a retired train engineer (Bologna has a huge railway yard), helps her with the maths: each tortellini should weigh 2 g; 1 kg (2 lb 4 oz) of filling makes 2 kg (4 lb 8 oz) of tortellini and you should allow between 40 and 50 tortellini per person (the extra ten are for second helpings). All this, and Cristina still does everything by eye – accurately.

Tortellini are a specialty of Bologna and, of course, there is an official recipe registered with the Bologna Chamber of Commerce, which says the filling should be equal quantities of pork loin, prosciutto, mortadella and Parmigiano Reggiano. Cristina's recipe doesn't adhere to this, and it was given to her by her grandmother, probably before the official version was written.

They are always delicious, whatever the variations, and form an essential part of Christmas celebrations – although they are eaten all year round these days. Gianni says they don't eat them very often, maybe once a week at Sunday lunch.

Making tortellini can be a tricky process; their tiny size requires nimble fingers and the sfoglia needs to stay soft and supple. Cristina uses plastic sheets to cover the dough while she works on a few at a time, and recalls that her mother used to use damp tea towels or work on a wet tablecloth to stop the pasta from drying out. She also recommends that if you are slow, to not roll out the dough all at once. Divide the dough into thirds, and if you find the squares are drying out, heap them together in a pile because then they dry out less quickly.

Ideally, make the filling the day before you want to use it as this gives the flavours a chance to mingle and settle in with one another. Bring the mixture to room temperature if you have placed it in the fridge overnight. Cristina says you can also leave the pasta dough in the fridge overnight, but bring it out 3 hours before you want to use it.

Recipe method overleaf

4 litres (1 gallon) meat stock (follow the
recipe on page 203, but Cristina says
not to peel the onion. She likes the
tawny colour the skins give the stock.
She also sticks 2 cloves into the
onion first)

FOR THE PASTA
500 g (1 lb 2 oz/4 cups) 00 flour or plain
(all-purpose) flour
5 eggs

FOR THE FILLING
230 g (8 oz) pork loin
100 g (3½ oz) prosciutto
230 g (8 oz) mortadella
100 g (3½ oz) grated Parmigiano
Reggiano (preferably aged for
30 months)
10 g (1 tablespoon) salt
1 egg
freshly grated nutmeg (to taste)

For the filling, mince the meats separately, as the textures are so different. You want a fine texture, similar to what you want when making meatballs. (My Italian butcher puts the meat three times through her mincer.) Combine them with the cheese, salt and egg to form a sturdy paste. Use your hands to squish everything together thoroughly and then poach or microwave a tiny bit to taste it; Cristina is happy to try hers raw. The seasoning should be punchy.

Make the pasta dough as described on page 18, and once rested roll it out (see Cristina's tips in the introduction). Cristina has a special roller which cuts lines 3 cm (1¼ in) apart. Alternatively, you could use a ruler and a sharp knife or smooth pastry cutter to slice your square pieces of pasta.

Dab small petit pois-sized lumps of filling into the centre of each square. Fold the edge over to make a triangle and squeeze the edges. Then, holding one small corner between your forefinger and thumb, wrap the other small corner around your forefinger, so the filling remains on the fingernail side and with the right angle of the tortellino pointing upwards. Squeeze the corners together to seal. Well done. You have 499 to go!

Place the tortellini on a tray. They can be left, covered with a tea towel for several hours. (You can also freeze them at this point, too. When it comes to serving them, simply cook them in the broth from frozen – do not thaw them first.)

Warm some soup bowls and bring the stock to a gentle simmer in a large pan. Add the tortellini and cook them until they float – about 3 minutes, or longer if they have been frozen. You will have to do this in batches if you are cooking them all. Have people waiting in line.

Ladle out 40 tortellini per person into the warmed soup bowls and congratulate yourself.

SARA'S PASSATELLI IN STOCK

FOR 4-6 PEOPLE

Passatelli are plump cheesy noodles made with breadcrumbs. They are a specialty of Emilia Romagna and northern Le Marche, in central Italy. They look a little like wriggly decrepit earthworms, but don't let that put you off. There are regional differences, of course: they are served in a meat stock inland, and a fish stock on the coast – where cooks add lemon zest to the dough instead of nutmeg. Traditionally, passatelli was a way of using up stale bread, so make sure yours is a few days old. Give it a blitz to make very fine crumbs, like sand in texture.

These days, passatelli are sometimes served as *pastasciutta*, i.e. with a condimento rather than in brodo. They are rather good with stewed courgette (zucchini), for example.

Using flour in this recipe is seen as an admission of defeat by some cooks, since the noodles should hold together without it. I have tried and failed to achieve a completely flourless passatelli noodle, and I blame it on the bread. Sara's tip is to test your passatelli by simmering a couple – if they don't stick together, add a little more flour to the mixture.

Sara's recipe is: for every one egg, use 40 g (1½ oz) finely ground breadcrumbs and 50 g (2 oz) grated Parmigiano Reggiano that has been aged for 24 months.

4 litres (1 gallon) meat stock
  (see page 203)

FOR THE PASTA
3 eggs, beaten
120 g (4¼ oz) stale, dry, fine
  breadcrumbs
150 g (5 oz) grated Parmigiano Reggiano,
  plus extra to serve
1 tablespoon plain (all-purpose) flour
½ teaspoon freshly grated nutmeg
  (or lemon zest)
¼ teaspoon salt

Mix all the pasta ingredients together, making sure it is a stiff, homogenous mass. Add more breadcrumbs if the mixture slumps. Cover it with a tea towel and leave it to rest for 30 minutes.

Bring your stock to a gentle simmer in a large saucepan. Slice off a piece of dough that will fit into your potato ricer and squeeze it through onto a plate. Take a pinch or two of your pasta dough and cook it in the stock. If they turn to polenta, knead a little more flour into the dough.

When you're happy with your dough, slice it into bits and feed them through the potato ricer. You want to create shortish noodles - about 7 cm (2¾ in) long - so cut them with scissors or a knife as they come through the ricer. Slide the noodles into the soup and simmer them until they bob to the surface - it will only take a couple of minutes. Test them after 1 minute.

Have warmed soup plates on standby and serve the soup immediately with extra grated Parmigiano Reggiano if you wish.

GINA'S MEAT RAVIOLI FROM PARMA

MAKES ABOUT 150 ANOLINI, ENOUGH FOR 8–10 PEOPLE

Anolini hail from the Parma and Piacenza areas of northern Italy. Cross the river Po and they become *marubini* in the Cremona region. They are little moon-shaped ravioli filled with a rich mixture of minced beef stew and Parmigiano Reggiano. Once, they were the preserve of aristocracy and the wealthy. Nowadays, families get together on Christmas Eve to assemble the anolini for their Christmas lunch.

Gina is an enthusiastic cook who regrets not taking the plunge and setting up her own restaurant in her youth. Instead, she loves to make pasta for family and friends.

This recipe will make more beef stew than you need, so keep it for another meal. You will need a circular ravioli stamp with a serrated edge, around 3 cm (1¼ in) in diameter. (If you don't have one, you could use a serrated-edged cookie cutter instead.)

4 litres (1 gallon) meat stock
(see page 203)

FOR THE PASTA
400 g (14 oz/3⅓ cups) 00 flour
or plain (all-purpose) flour
4 eggs

FOR THE BEEF FILLING
15 g (½ oz) butter
1 onion, diced
500 g (1 lb 2 oz) beef shoulder, diced
2 carrots, diced
2 celery sticks, diced
2 cloves
2 sprigs thyme
½ bottle red wine
100 g (3½ oz) breadcrumbs
1 egg
200 g (7 oz) grated Parmigiano Reggiano
freshly grated nutmeg (to taste)
salt

To make the filling, melt the butter in a casserole and soften the onion, then add the beef, vegetables, cloves, thyme, wine and a teaspoon of salt. Cover the pan and cook the beef over a low heat for around 3 hours. Top up with water when necessary. Once cooked, the beef should be tender enough to mash with a fork. Allow to cool.

Blitz 200 g (7 oz) of the cooked beef in a food processor, then add the remaining ingredients for the filling with around 50–100 ml (1¾–3½ fl oz/ 3 tablespoons–scant ½ cup) beef stock from the stew (enough to bring the mixture together). Season with salt and blitz again to form a stiff, smooth paste. Gina likes to leave this overnight for the flavour to develop – she starts the anolini process two days before she makes them.

Make the pasta dough as described on page 18. Roll out your sfoglia about 1 mm thick – and cut it into broad strips about 8 cm (3¼ in) wide. Keep them covered with a tea towel to stop them from drying. Place large green olive-sized pieces of the beef filling along the length of one half of a dough strip at 6 cm (2½ in) intervals. Fold the other half of the dough over the filling and tap it down by curling your fingers and using the side of your hand to surround the filling. You want to exclude the air to stop the anolini puffing up when they are cooking. Use a ravioli stamp to press out circular ravioli. Keep them spread out on a tray while you work your way through the rest of the pasta and filling. Bits of cut-out pasta can be squished together and re-rolled.

Bring the meat stock to a gentle simmer in a pan. Lower the anolini into it and cook for 3–5 minutes. Serve the anolini in bowls with some of the stock.

ANNA'S DUCHESS' LITTLE SNAILS

———

FOR 4 PEOPLE

We had originally visited Anna Faggi to film *cresc'tajat*, but then she said, 'Would you like me to make *Lumachelle della Duchessa*?' So, of course, I said yes. How could one not be interested in a pasta with such a wonderful name?

Duchess' Little Snails is a special dish from the Pesaro and Urbino region of central Italy. The 'snails' are delicate, tiny ridged tubes of cinnamon-scented pasta – a bit like mini *garganelli* (see page 161). Anna says, 'This pasta is rarely made because it's so labour intensive. But it dates back to the 15th century and the ingredients, like the cinnamon, would have been very expensive – so this was a special occasion dish, even for a Duchess.'

That special occasion was the birth of a child. Noblewomen were expected to rest for 40 days after childbirth. To build up their strength, they were given this dish; the pasta for which was made by enclosed orders of nuns in the area – they were the only group of people with the time to dedicate to the process. The original dish was these little pasta snails served in capon stock and garnished with chicken entrails, specifically the stomachs. This was considered the absolutely best thing to feed an aristocratic new mother.

Anna says, 'If you don't feel like making the snails, then simply cut the sfoglia into *quadrucci* – little squares – it will taste the same.' If you like pasta projects, you will need a garganelli/cavatelli paddle and rod to make this pasta. And quite a lot of time! Anna, in fact, uses a weaving comb, called a *pettine*, and the stem of bulrush to make hers.

1 litre (34 fl oz/4 cups) decent meat or chicken stock (see page 203 or 238)

FOR THE PASTA
200 g (7 oz/1²/₃ cups) 0 flour or plain (all-purpose) flour
10 g (½ oz) grated Parmigiano Reggiano
1 teaspoon ground cinnamon
½ teaspoon nutmeg, freshly grated
½ teaspoon black pepper
2 eggs

TO SERVE
grated Parmigiano Reggiano (not chicken stomachs!)

Mix the flour with the cheese and spices. Swirl a well in the middle and add the eggs. Then make the pasta dough as described on page 18. After it has rested for 30 minutes, roll it out thin enough so you can see the pasta board through it – about 1 mm.

Cut the sfoglia into pappardelle – 2 cm (¾ in) wide strips. Take a strip and wrap one end round the garganelli rod once to make a little tube. Snip the rest of the strip off and press the ends of the tube together to seal. Repeat this along the rod – you will probably only fit about two snails.

Gently roll the rod and tubes along the garganelli paddle to create little ridges on them. Cajole them from the rod onto a tray and continue until you have used all your strips of dough.

Warm some soup bowls and bring your stock to a simmer in a large saucepan. Add the snails and cook them for 1–2 minutes. Taste one to check for doneness, then ladle the soup into the bowls. Scatter a little Parmigiano Reggiano over each serving. Remember to inhale deeply before eating – the cinnamon gives this the most wonderful aroma and flavour.

VELIA'S CAPPELLETTI IN STOCK

FOR 4 PEOPLE

Velia and her husband, Venanzo, live in the neighbouring village to mine and I often see them working on their farm. The earthquakes of 2016 forced them to move into the village, but they still return every day to their home a kilometre down the road. This is where Venanzo was born and grew up, overlooking Lake Cingoli, with the snow-capped (for half the year) Sibillini mountains beyond. They grow a little bit of everything: a couple of rows of vines, free-range chickens and geese, beans and courgettes (zucchini). And from it, Velia can see the house where she was born on the other side of the lake.

Velia worked for many years in a clothes factory making uniforms. Her job was to iron the finished clothes and she needed a stool to stand on to do this. Her other job was as a cook for a nearby *osteria* – also owned by the factory boss, and where most of the staff used to eat. She'd clock off and go and cook lunch! Not surprisingly, Velia is an excellent cook, although meat is a special treat that she eats rarely; she loves the vegetables from her garden too much. These days she makes cappelletti for a local restaurant, Lo Smeraldo – The Emerald – which pretty much describes the colour of the lake.

Every family in the Le Marche region has its own recipe for cappelletti. Some cooks add rosemary, garlic and/or white wine to the meat mixture when cooking, but Velia likes to keep her flavours simple. *Cappelletti marchigiani* are similar but not the same as the tortellini from Bologna (see page 209). The filling is different, with the inclusion of turkey.

For the best texture, Velia says you should use a meat mincer. She has a hand-cranked one, but you can also get a gadget which attaches to your food mixer. Use a food processor if you must, but be careful not to turn the meat into a paste. Some cappelletti are made as pasta circles but Velia prefers squares, as there is less pasta waste. She uses a ruler to ensure the cappelletti are all the same size; they should be about 3 cm (1¼ in) square. The filling can be made the day before if you prefer. Cappelletti also freezes successfully, so you can do this well in advance of Christmas Eve when this dish is traditionally served. Add to hot stock from frozen and simmer for a little longer.

Recipe photo overleaf

3 litres (101 fl oz/12²/₃ cups) meat stock
  (see page 203)

FOR THE PASTA
400 g (14 oz/3¹/₃ cups) 00 flour or plain
  (all-purpose) flour
4 eggs

FOR THE FILLING
200 g (7 oz) turkey breast
200 g (7 oz) lean pork loin steak
150 g (7 oz) beef (or veal) steak
1 tablespoon butter
1 fresh Italian sausage, skin removed,
  meat crumbled
1 thick slice of mortadella
1 egg, beaten
100 g (3¹/₂ oz) grated Parmigiano
  Reggiano
¹/₂ teaspoon freshly grated nutmeg
salt

TO SERVE
grated Parmigiano Reggiano

Cut the turkey, pork and beef (or veal) into smallish chunks. Heat a large frying pan (skillet) and melt the butter. Once it is sizzling, add the chopped meat and sausage (except the mortadella) and sauté it until cooked, adding a little water (or wine if you prefer) to stop it from burning. Leave the meat to cool.

Once cool, mince all the meats, along with the mortadella, so the mixture is finely ground but not a paste. Then squish in the egg, Parmigiano Reggiano and nutmeg. The filling will be stiff. Taste the mixture and adjust for salt – don't under-season, otherwise the result will be bland.

Make the pasta dough as described on page 18. Roll out the dough until it is thin enough that you could see a tablecloth pattern beneath it. Use a pastry cutter and a ruler to cut a grid of 3 cm (1¼ in) squares. Keep the sfoglia covered to stop it from drying out while you make the cappelletti.

Pop a pea-sized piece of filling into the centre of each square. Fold the pasta over to make a triangle and press the edges firmly together. Hold one of the smaller corners between your finger and thumb and bring the other small corner down so the two corners meet. These two corners should be pointing away from the top corner. Squeeze the points together. It looks a bit like bringing a scarf under someone's chin. *Ecco!* Your first cappelletto. Repeat several hundred times more. In fact, it's a good idea to get friends and family involved at this stage.

Warm some soup bowls and bring your stock to a simmer in a large saucepan. Simmer the cappelletti for around 5 minutes – taste one or two to check for doneness. Serve, steaming hot, with a snowfall of Parmigiano Reggiano rapidly melting into the liquid.

eight

Ravioli and tortelli

Food historians tell us ravioli and tortelli – stuffed pasta – have been around since the 16th century. Ravioli can be round, semi-circular, square or triangular, whereas tortelli can be this, plus other shapes as well. In this chapter, the focus is on ravioli and tortelli served with butter - which is only used for cooking in northern Italy and some parts of central Italy.

VANDA'S CAPPELLACCI WITH PUMPKIN

———

FOR 6 PEOPLE

Cappellacci di zucca are a speciality of the Ferrara region of Emilia Romagna. They are hat-shaped ravioli filled with a pumpkin purée.

Vanda Soncini, her daughter Maria Grazia and granddaughter Elettra work in their family restaurant, La Capanna di Eraclio (Eraclio's Hut) in the wilds of the Po Delta. This cappellacci recipe is something she makes for high days and holidays. The extra egg yolk adds richness to the dough. You could also use 400 g (14 oz/ 3⅓ cups) of plain (all-purpose) flour if you prefer – but the addition of the semolina adds a bit of 'bite' to the dough. If you'd prefer or it's easier to find, butternut squash is a good substitute here – in which case it can be baked without the salt.

FOR THE PASTA
200 g (7 oz/1⅔ cups) 00 flour or plain (all-purpose) flour
200 g (7 oz/1⅔ cups) finely ground semolina flour
4 eggs, plus 1 egg yolk

FOR THE FILLING
1 large pumpkin, cut into 6 large chunks
coarse sea salt
¼ teaspoon freshly grated nutmeg
100 g (3½ oz) grated Parmigiano Reggiano
salt and pepper

TO SERVE
120 g (4 oz) butter
a generous amount of fresh, torn sage leaves
grated Parmigiano Reggiano

Make the pasta dough as described on page 18. Let it rest. Preheat the oven to 160°C (320°F/gas 2).

Cut the pumpkin into large pieces and remove the seeds. Weigh out 1 kg (2 lb 4 oz) and keep the rest for another dish. Cover a baking tray with a layer of coarse sea salt – this helps to absorb the moisture. Place the pumpkin pieces on the tray and bake for about 30–40 minutes, until the flesh is soft. Cool, then remove the peel from the pulp. Mash the pumpkin – Vanda says it helps to sieve it to get rid of any lumps and stringy bits – then stir in the nutmeg and Parmigiano Reggiano. Make sure the cheese is thoroughly mixed in and season it well. Set aside while you make the pasta.

Roll out the dough to a thickness of 1 mm – you should be able to see your hand through it. Use a pastry cutter or knife to cut 7 cm (2¾ in) squares. Place a teaspoon of the filling in the centre of each pasta square.

To make a cappellaccio, fold the pasta over the filling to make a triangle. Hold one of the smaller corners between your finger and thumb and bring the opposite corner around your forefinger so the two corners meet and create the hat. Make sure the edges are firmly pressed together. Once made, place each one on a tray covered with a cloth and sprinkled with semolina. Continue until all the ingredients are used.

Bring a large pan of salted water to the boil. In another large pan, melt the butter over a gentle heat and add the sage leaves, allowing them to crisp up.

Once the water has reached a simmer, cook the cappellacci for around 4 minutes and taste one for doneness. Continue to cook for another minute or so if necessary. Drain the pasta carefully and add them to the butter pan and continue to cook for another minute.

To serve, gently scoop the pasta into 6 bowls, dividing the buttery sauce equally between them. Scatter over some freshly grated Parmigiano Reggiano and serve.

This recipe has several stages to it, but it's not difficult – although actually making the cappellacci takes some practice. It's also something to get the whole family doing.

MONICA'S PASTA BASKETS WITH RICOTTA AND LEMON

MAKES 32 CESTINI, ENOUGH FOR
4 PEOPLE, AS A STARTER

Monica Venturi and her sister, Daniela, own a pasta shop behind the central covered market in Bologna. Their father was in the meat trade and good food has always been a central part of their lives, but it wasn't until they were middle-aged that they decided to open the shop. 'It was a natural progression for us. We love pasta and so we decided to make it full time.'

Monica says, 'When you make pasta for a living, rolling out a beautiful circle of dough doesn't make sense – it's more efficient to make a long, wide strip and let it drop off the edge of the table. That is what you will see professional *sfogline*, the pasta-making ladies, doing all over Bologna. We may make the dough using a food mixer because our quantities are so large, but we are never tempted by a pasta-rolling machine. The resulting sfoglia just doesn't have the right texture.

'Daniela and I invented *cestini* – pasta baskets – for our shop because we wanted to offer something different. I don't know if this is the right word for them because I'm sure other people have thought of this shape, too. We think it's nice and elegant, and it's what I like to make on Sunday when I'm "on holiday" from our pasta business!'

FOR THE PASTA
300 g (10½ oz/scant 2½ cups) 00 flour
or plain (all-purpose) flour
3 eggs

FOR THE FILLING
250 g (9 oz) ricotta, drained weight
70 g (2½ oz) grated Parmigiano Reggiano
zest of 1 unwaxed large lemon

TO SERVE
30 g (1 oz) butter
2 teaspoons ground cinnamon

Make the pasta as described on page 18. Roll it out to about 1 mm thick, so you can see the board beneath it. Cut into 7 cm (2¾ in) squares. Monica has a special roller to do this, but you can use a ruler and a pastry cutter.

Combine all the ingredients to make the filling. Dot a teaspoon of the ricotta mixture into the centre of each square. Gather the 4 points together and firmly press the adjoining edges together to create 4 seams. Repeat until you have used all your filling.

Bring a large pan of salted water to a gentle canter of a simmer and lower the cestini into it with a small sieve or slotted spoon. Cook for 3–4 minutes. While they are cooking, melt the butter in a small pan. When the cestini are ready, don't drain them, but scoop them out with a sieve or slotted spoon and plate them up with a couple of spoonfuls of melted butter and a dusting of cinnamon. Allow about 8 per person.

GIUSY'S CASONCELLI FROM BARBARIGA

**MAKES ENOUGH FOR
10 PEOPLE**

Learning all the names for Italian pasta can be very confusing, as the same name can be given to different types, and one shape can be called several different names depending which area it comes from. *Casoncelli* comes from the former category: in Barbariga, a village in Lombardy, south of Lake Iseo, they are untwisted, sweet-wrapper style, while 25 kilometres (15 miles) away in the city of Brescia, casoncelli are clog-shoe shaped. They have been made since the 16th century, and the mixture of meats tells you this pasta was a way of using up leftovers. *Casoncelli di Barbariga* now have an official recipe, which Giusy demonstrated for us.

Her sage leaves and spinach came from her backyard, which is totally devoted to vegetables, lovingly tended by her husband. Persuade your friends to help you; these are easy to make, and they are a good excuse for a party.

FOR THE PASTA
500 g (1 lb 2 oz/4 cups) 00 flour
   or plain (all-purpose) flour
4 eggs, plus 2 egg yolks

FOR THE FILLING
200 g (7 oz) spinach
2 teaspoons butter
150 g (5 oz) pork loin, cubed
150 g (5 oz) ham, sliced into ribbons
200 g (7 oz) breadcrumbs
150 g (5 oz) grated Parmigiano Reggiano
   or Grana Padan
freshly grated nutmeg (to taste)
about 50 ml (1¾ fl oz/3 tablespoons)
   meat stock (see page 203), to bind
   everything together
salt

TO SERVE
100 g (3½ oz) butter
10 sage leaves
grated Parmigiano Reggiano

Make the dough as described on page 18. Let the dough rest.

Blanch the spinach for 1 minute in a pan of boiling water. Drain it through a sieve and squeeze out the excess water. You will end up with 100 g (3½ oz) cooked spinach. Heat the butter in a frying pan (skillet) and gently sauté the pork until it cooks through but doesn't brown. In a food processor, blitz the pork with the spinach and ham to make a rough paste. Season with salt.

Mix the breadcrumbs, cheese and nutmeg together. Stir in the meat and spinach mixture, and add a little meat stock to bind everything together. It should hold together when you roll it into a ball. Leave it cool. Taste and adjust the seasoning.

Divide the pasta dough in half and roll out 2 sfoglia sheets about 1 mm thick – 2 pieces are easier to manage. Cut the sheets into 7 cm (2¾ in) squares using a ruler and knife or pastry cutter.

To assemble the casoncelli, place a green olive-sized piece of the filling into the centre of each square. Look at each square as a diamond, take the point closest to you and roll it over, around the filling, making sure the pasta point furthest from you stays underneath (it shouldn't actually move from the pasta board). Press down firmly on either side of the filling. Repeat until you have used up all the filling or pasta – whichever comes first.

Warm a serving platter and bring a large saucepan of salted water to the boil. Cook the pasta in batches, for around 5 minutes, placing the cooked pasta on the warmed platter.

To serve, melt the butter in a frying pan and sauté the sage leaves until they release lovely aromas, then pour this over the casoncelli, sprinkle on the cheese and eat immediately.

LEONDINA'S NETTLE TORTELLI

MAKES ABOUT 90 TORTELLI,
ENOUGH FOR 6-8 PEOPLE

Leondina lives in the hills to the south of Faenza, in Emilia-Romagna, on the way to Florence. When early morning mist swathes the valleys and obscures modern buildings, all one can see are pert hills and the occasional tiny church with a tall spire on top. It looks pretty much the same as it did 300 years ago. Leondina grew up here with her seven siblings. Her mum came from Abruzzo, so Leondina loved *spaghetti al pomodoro* as a child. 'We used to make tagliatelle, but of course we used fewer eggs because we were poorer then.' Now, for her family on Sundays, she makes pasta dishes like cannelloni filled with ricotta and ham and dressed with béchamel sauce and a little bit of ragù.

'The success of tortelli d'ortica,' says Leondina, 'depends on the quality of your ingredients. Usually I make my own ricotta; I like sheep's milk ricotta for flavour and cow's milk for texture – so I use a mixture. I always buy Parmigiano Reggiano that has been aged at least for 24 months for this dish.'

Wear plastic gloves to pick your nettles – once cooked they no longer sting. Leondina doesn't bother with protection though, she just grasps them firmly. The tortelli can be frozen successfully – cook them straight from the freezer.

Only pick young growing nettles in early spring for this recipe. At other times of the year, use spinach.

FOR THE PASTA
120 g (4 oz) fresh nettles (or spinach)
3 eggs
1 tablespoon extra-virgin olive oil
400 g (14 oz/3⅓ cups) 00 flour or
    plain (all-purpose) flour
semolina flour, for dusting

FOR THE FILLING
500 g (1 lb 2 oz) ricotta (sheep or cow's
    or a 50/50 mixture), drained weight
150 g (5 oz) nettles or spinach
125 g (4 oz) grated Parmigiano Reggiano
    (preferably aged for 24 months)
freshly grated nutmeg (to taste)
salt

TO SERVE
60 g (2 oz) butter
18 sage leaves
grated Parmigiano Reggiano

First make your pasta. Bring a large saucepan of water to the boil, then blanch the nettles for 30 seconds. Scoop them out and drain them through a sieve, then rinse the leaves under cold water. Squeeze out the water. The resulting weight of the nettles should be 60 g (2 oz). Put this in a blender with the eggs and oil and blitz together into a gloriously green liquid. It's the colour of spring.

Make a mound of flour on your pasta board (or do this in a large bowl). Create a well in the middle and pour in the green liquid. Use your hands to bring everything together, then start kneading. Knead your dough for around 15 minutes, until it is completely smooth. Cover with a tea towel (or put it in a lidded bowl) and let it rest for 30 minutes while you prepare the filling.

Sheep's milk ricotta has a tendency towards wateriness, so if you are using it, make sure to drain your ricotta in a sieve first. Blanch the nettles or spinach for the filling as you did for the pasta dough, squeezing the water out as thoroughly as possible. It should weigh about 90 g (3 oz) after squeezing. Chop it finely, then mix with the ricotta and Parmigiano Reggiano. Grate in some nutmeg and add a pinch of salt. Taste and adjust the seasoning, adding more of either if you think it needs it.

Have a tray dusted with semolina at the ready. Roll the dough out in batches to about 1–2 mm thickness. Cut the dough into 6–7 cm (2½–2¾ in) squares, then put a walnut-sized blob of filling into the middle of each square. These tortelli are a triangle shape, so take one corner of the square and fold it over diagonally. Press the edges to seal it. (Leondina uses the edge of a ravioli stamp to do this.) Place each tortello on the tray and repeat until you have used up all of the filling.

To cook the tortelli, bring a large saucepan of salted water to the boil then gently plop in the tortelli. Cook them for 3–4 minutes, tasting one to check if they're done. Meanwhile, in another pan, melt the butter then add the sage. Use a slotted spoon or sieve to lift the cooked pasta from the water and into the butter. Gently toss the pasta with the butter and sage, adding a few tablespoons of cheese to help emulsify everything. Serve immediately with more cheese on top, if you like.

CLAUDIA'S TORTELLI D'ERBETTA

MAKES 60 TORTELLI, ENOUGH FOR 4 PEOPLE AS A MAIN COURSE

Parma is where every food lover should go if they are visiting Italy. It's the centre for *prosciutto di Parma* and Parmigiano Reggiano cheese, and balsamic vinegar is made just down the road in Modena. And its inhabitants, naturally enough, expect very high standards of its food. *Pastifici* (pasta shops) can be found in every neighbourhood and Claudia Gazza, in her retirement, helps her daughter Carlotta run one. *Tortelli d'erbetta* are a speciality of Parma, and it's one of Claudia's favourites to make. She likes to use ricotta made from whole milk to make the filling richer. The greens can vary (in the countryside cooks may forage for nettles, for example) but Claudia prefers Swiss chard for year-round reliability.

FOR THE PASTA
400 g (14 oz/3⅓ cups) 00 flour
    or plain (all-purpose) flour
4 eggs
semolina flour, for dusting

FOR THE FILLING
170 g (6 oz) Swiss chard leaves, stems
    removed
550 g (1 lb 3 oz) ricotta, drained weight
60 g (2 oz) grated Parmigiano Reggiano
    (preferably aged for 24 months)
freshly grated nutmeg (to taste)
salt

TO SERVE
50 g (2 oz) unsalted butter
50 g (2 oz) grated Parmigiano Reggiano
    (preferably aged for 24 months)

Make the pasta dough as described on page 18. Claudia says, 'You know when you have kneaded the dough enough because you will find little holes in it.'

To make the filling, bring a large saucepan of water to the boil and cook the Swiss chard leaves for 3–4 minutes, until wilted. Scoop them out into a sieve and rinse under cold water. Squeeze out as much excess water as possible; you should be left with around 150 g (5 oz) cooked greens. Chop the chard quite finely. Claudia recommends using a mezzaluna so the chard retains some texture.

In a large mixing bowl, combine the chopped chard, ricotta and Parmigiano Reggiano. Grate in plenty of nutmeg and season with salt, to taste.

Divide the dough into quarters and roll one piece out into a long strip about 10 cm (4 in) wide, dusting with semolina flour to prevent sticking. Cover the pieces of dough you are not using to prevent them drying out. Dot walnut-sized spoonfuls of the filling in a line down one long edge of each strip, roughly 2 cm (¾ in) from the edge, and leaving about 5 cm (2 in) between them. Fold each strip over lengthways to cover the fillings and line up the edges. Working from the middle outwards, use your hands to press the pasta down carefully around each bit of filling to seal it, making sure to push out any trapped air.

Using a knife or a pasta cutter, trim the top (unfolded) edge and two sides around each bit of filling, leaving a border of dough (a scant 1 cm/½ in) around each one. Repeat these steps until you've used up all of the filling. If you have any leftover scraps of pasta, keep them to use in soups.

Bring a large pot of salted water to a simmer and cook the tortelli for about 5 minutes – they will float to the surface and puff up slightly. You may need to do this in batches. While they're cooking, melt the butter in a sauté pan. Use a slotted spoon to lift the cooked tortelli from the water and into the pan with the butter, swirling them gently so that the butter and pasta water start to emulsify.

Plate them up with spoonfuls of butter, and scatter over generous amounts of Parmigiano Reggiano.

*The tortelli should drown in butter
and dry with the Parmigiano.
Be generous with both!*

MARIA'S RAVIOLI INCACIATI

MAKES ENOUGH FOR 12–14 PEOPLE

The Sibillini Mountains hug Ascoli Piceno like a shoulder shrug. It's a charming town and the surrounding area is home to several pasta specialities. *Ravioli incaciati* is one example.

Ravioli incaciati means 'full of cheese', although the filling is actually a mixture of chicken, pork and cheese, spiced with cinnamon and a little nutmeg. They're traditionally served at *Carnevale*, the beginning of Lent, and Maria, like most housewives in the area, makes huge quantities for the celebration. She says, 'I don't measure anything – it's all done by eye. My mother taught me and that's how I make them. Every family has their own recipe for these.'

The dialect name is *ravioli di pappa* because the filling is mushy (*pappa* means baby food). 'You should be able to stir the filling with a wooden spoon,' says Maria. We filmed her making these in her summer kitchen, a small building next to her large *orto* (vegetable garden), because the 2016 earthquakes had rendered her home unsafe, like so many in the area. The ravioli can be frozen – cook them straight from the freezer.

FOR THE CHICKEN STOCK
1.7 kg (3 lb 11 oz) free-range organic chicken
1 stick cinnamon

FOR THE PASTA
500 g (1 lb 2 oz/4 cups) 00 flour or plain (all-purpose) flour
5 eggs

FOR THE FILLING
4 tablespoons extra-virgin olive oil
100 g (3½ oz) pork loin, diced
100 ml (3½ fl oz/scant ½ cup) white wine
flesh from the cooked chicken (from the stock)
200 g (7 oz) stale bread, crusts removed
freshly grated nutmeg (to taste)
2 teaspoons freshly ground cinnamon
200 g (7 oz) grated Parmigiano Reggiano (preferably aged for 24 or 36 months) or aged Pecorino
2 eggs
salt

TO SERVE
30 g (1 oz) butter
30 g (1 oz) grated Parmigiano Reggiano or Pecorino
pinch of ground cinnamon

Make the stock: put the chicken in a large pot, add the cinnamon and cover with water. Bring to the boil, then lower the heat and simmer for 1 hour. Let it cool in the stock. Once cool enough to handle, strip the meat from the bones and reserve the stock.

While it is cooling, make the pasta as described on page 18. While it rests for 30 minutes, make the filling.

Heat the olive oil in a frying pan (skillet) and sauté the pork for about 10 minutes, deglazing the pan with a little white wine. Place it a food processor with the cooked chicken and blitz the meats together. You want it to resemble a crumble topping.

Place the slices of bread in a large bowl and sprinkle over some grated nutmeg and a little bit of cinnamon. Ladle over enough chicken stock to make the bread properly wet through, but not drowning.

Stir in the meat mixture and the cheese. Beat the eggs and stir these in, too. If it's very stiff add a little more stock. You're aiming for a thick paste – remember it should be mushy, not stiff. Taste it, and then add pinches of salt, ground cinnamon and nutmeg until you have something that is well seasoned. (Wrapping the filling in a pasta always knocks back the flavour a bit, so don't be timid.)

Roll out the dough to a thickness of about 1–2 mm. Cut the sfoglia into 12 cm (5 in) wide strips. Place apricot-sized dumplings of filling at 10 cm (4 in) intervals along one long edge of each strip, about 2 cm (¾ in) from the edge. Fold the dough over to cover the filling, and tap down around each mound,

cupping your hands and using the sides of your palms, to remove the air.

Using a fluted pastry cutter, cut around each portion to make half-moon-shaped ravioli, where the pasta fold is the straight side. Place them curved side up on your board and crimp the curved edge as you would a Cornish pasty – the frill is meant to resemble a cockscomb. Don't be alarmed if they look large – these are quite big ravioli. Arrange the ravioli

incaciati on floured trays while you complete the rest. You can choose to freeze them now, if you wish.

Warm a serving platter and bring a large saucepan of salted water to the boil. Cook the ravioli for 6–7 minutes. They are ready when they bob to the surface of the water. While they are cooking, melt the butter in a small pan with the cheese and cinnamon. Arrange the cooked ravioli on the platter and pour the butter sauce over the top.

IDA'S AGNOLOTTI DEL PLIN

FOR 6-8 PEOPLE

Ida's recipe for agnolotti del plin is really a variation on her recipe for Tajarin with roast meat gravy on page 170 – instead of making a ribbon pasta, you make baby ravioli. Tajarin utilises leftover gravy, while this recipe originally used leftover meat, hence the fillings vary widely across Piedmont. The three-meat style of Ida's is common in the Asti region of Piedmont, where she lives. Ida uses spinach, but other cooks use cabbage; what they are all doing here is being frugal and not throwing away their vegetables! We are cooking everything from scratch in this recipe, so it is quite long, but feel free to use your own leftovers.

Ida recommends using a manual grinder for mincing the meat, as it creates a lighter texture for the filling.

FOR THE PASTA
400 g (14 oz/3⅓ cups) 00 flour
4 eggs

FOR THE FILLING
30 g (1 oz) risotto rice
100 ml (3½ fl oz/scant ½ cup) milk
    or meat stock (see page 203)
35 g (1¼ oz) butter
100 g (3½ oz) spinach
2 garlic cloves
200 g (7 oz) pork shoulder, diced
200 g (7 oz) rose veal or beef shoulder,
    diced
200 g (7 oz) rabbit leg, diced
1 sprig of rosemary
75 ml (2½ fl oz/5 tablespoons) white
    wine
1 egg, beaten
150 g (5 oz) grated Parmigiano Reggiano
freshly grated nutmeg (to taste)
salt

TO SERVE
30 g (1 oz) butter
plenty of sage leaves
grated Parmigiano Reggiano

Make the dough as described on page 18.

While the pasta is resting, simmer the risotto rice in the milk or stock for about 18 minutes – you are not trying to make risotto, but simply to cook the rice. (Check the packet for the exact time.) It should still be a little firm but not crunchy.

Melt a tablespoon of the butter in a frying pan (skillet) and sauté the spinach with a whole garlic clove, until the leaves have collapsed and reduced considerably in volume. Keep cooking it until all the liquid has evaporated. Remove the garlic and mix the spinach into the rice, then leave it to cool.

Trim the meat of any gristle and fat. Melt the rest of the butter on a medium heat, then add the second garlic clove and cook for a minute or so. Add the meat and brown on all sides before adding the rosemary and a little of the wine. Keep adding the wine as it evaporates when necessary – you may not need all of it. Depending on the size you've chopped your meat, it should take about 10 minutes to cook. Leave the mixture to cool slightly. Then use a meat grinder or the pulse setting of your food processor to mince it. (Reserve the meat juices to dress the pasta, if you wish.) Add the spinach and rice mixture and mince or pulse that, too. It should be a nice crumbly texture, not a smooth paste. Mash in the beaten egg, cheese and nutmeg. Season with salt. Taste the mixture – wrapping the filling in pasta always knocks the flavour back a little, so make sure it's good and savoury.

Roll out your dough so you can read a letter through it – it should be about 1 mm thick. Cut into strips about 12 cm (5 in) wide. Keep the rest of the strips covered while you make the agnolotti.

Dot half-teaspoon-sized amounts of the filling at 5 cm (2 in) intervals in a row, just in from one long edge of the pasta strip. Fold the pasta and filling over and pat out all the air around the filling, pressing along the long edges to seal the pasta. Cut along the strip with a pastry cutter so you have a single rope of filled pasta. Pinch the pasta between each pocket of filling with your thumb and forefinger – don't press down – to create ridges. *Plin* means pinch.

Drive your pastry cutter through each pinch, just a few millimetres either side of the filling. This will fold

the pasta over on each side of the filling to make a neat, tight parcel and to give it its distinctive look (I think the folds look like little ears). The ravioli should be 2–3 cm (1–1¼ in) long. Repeat this process until you have used up all your filling. (Watch Ida's video to bring these instructions to life!)

Bring a large pan of salted water to the boil and pour in your agnolotti. Once the pan has returned to the boil, cook the pasta for 5 minutes or so – taste one to test. Drain them thoroughly.

Melt the butter in a frying pan over a gently heat and bathe the sages leaves in it for a few minutes. Plate up the pasta and spoon the butter over each serving. Finish with some grated Parmigiano Reggiano.

Instead of melted butter you could use the gravy juices from stewing the meat mixture as a dressing.

GRAZIE! GRAZIE!

It's my name on the front cover, but Pasta Grannies is a group effort. Firstly, it wouldn't be possible without the wonderful women (and men) who welcome me into their kitchens – there are nearly 300 of them starring on the YouTube channel – *grazie di cuore.*

Thanks to the people who help me with the channel: Livia De Giovanni, Charlie Williams, Andrea Neri, Amanda Villa-Lobos, Heliana Trovato, Julia and Pino Ficara, Gianluca Giorgi, Megan Macqueen, Henry Bennison, Olivia Williamson, Gerry Diebel.

Thanks to myriad folk who have helped along the way: Paolo Arrigo and his family, Hana Asbrink, Paolo Bellantuoni, Alessandro Bravi and his nonna Maria, Maria Pia Castelli and husband Enrico, Monica Cesarato, Adam Chervis, Carmelo Chiaramonte, Jon Elek, Ettore Favini, Fabbio Ferrara, Ursula Ferrigno, Renzo Ibba, Renata, Raffaele and Valentina Giacobazzi, Caimin Jones, Michelle Lovric, Mort and Simona Mirghavameddin, Marina O'Loughlin, Nick Patten, Anders Sodergen, Wendell Steavenson, Carla Tomasi, Alexis Tymon, Marco Carini, Mario Ferrara and Karima Moyer Nocchi.

The fabulous Hardie Grant team: Kajal Mistry, Kate Pollard, Stephen King, Eila Purvis, Emma Marijewycz, Laura Willis, Laura Eldridge, Ruth Tewkesbury. The wonderful shoot team: Emma Lee, Indi Petrucci, Marina Filippelli, Kitty Coles, Imogen Wok. The talented team of designers: Clare Skeats, Evi O and Susan Le.

My mum, Sue, for being the extra pair of hands and the original Pasta Granny; my dad, Hugh, who was my wise counsel and biggest fan, inspired me to be ever curious and have lifelong adventures. And last but not least, my husband, Billy Macqueen, without whom those adventures would be no fun at all.

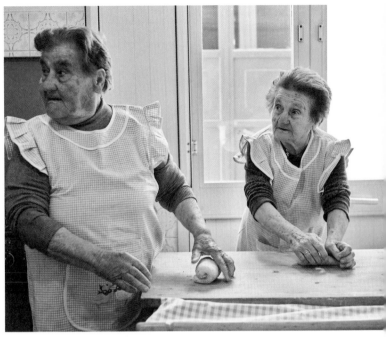

INDEX

Published in 2019 by Hardie Grant Books,
an imprint of Hardie Grant Publishing

Hardie Grant Books (London)
5th & 6th Floors
52–54 Southwark Street
London SE1 1UN

Hardie Grant Books (Melbourne)
Building 1, 658 Church Street
Richmond, Victoria 3121

hardiegrantbooks.com

British Library Cataloguing-in-Publication Data. A catalogue record
for this book is available from the British Library.

Pasta Grannies
ISBN: 978-1-78488-288-4

Publishing Director: Kate Pollard
Commissioning Editor: Kajal Mistry
Junior Editor: Eila Purvis
Editor: Laura Herring
Proofreader: Eve Marleau
Designer: Clare Skeats
Cover, Chapter Openers and Booklet Design:
    Evi O. Studio | Evi O & Susan Le
Photographer: Emma Lee
Photography Assistant: Indi Petrucci
Food Stylist: Marina Filippelli
Food Stylist Assistants: Kitty Coles and Imogen Wok
Prop Stylist: Tabitha Hawkins
Recipe Tester: Olivia Williamson
Pasta Maker: Julia Ficara
Indexer: Cathy Heath

Colour reproduction by p2d
Printed and bound in China by Leo Paper Products Ltd.